MARRIAGE
CENTERED
MONEY

Get on the Same Financial Page
and Achieve Your Life Goals *Together*

BILL NELSON, CFP®, CFT-I™

DISCLAIMER

The contents of this book are to be used only for educational purposes and are not designed to be a definitive guide on the subject matters therein. While this book is intended to educate couples in topics related to money and marriage, there are many topics in these fields that are outside the scope of this book. If you are experiencing financial abuse, financial infidelity, bankruptcy, fraud, or any other serious financial or marital issue, you should immediately seek help from a competent professional.

The information in this book does not constitute financial advice, legal advice, tax advice, or marriage advice, and there is no guarantee that the methods suggested in this book will be successful. Seek help from an experienced professional for professional assistance in these areas as needed.

All of the stories in this book are written based on what I've learned working with couples over the past five years but do not describe any specific person or couple. All stories in this book, including names, characters, events, and discussions, are used in a fictitious manner to convey real-life lessons and principles. Any resemblance to specific individuals or couples is entirely coincidental.

Although the publisher and the author have made every effort to confirm that the information in this book was complete and correct at the time of publication, the publisher and the author assume no responsibility for errors, omissions, or other inconsistencies herein and disclaim any liability to any party for any damage caused by errors or omissions.

Pacesetter Planning LLC is an Investment Adviser registered with the states of Virginia, Massachusetts, and California (as of the time of publication). Registration does not imply a certain level of skill or training. This book shall not be directly or indirectly interpreted as a solicitation of investment advisory services to persons of another jurisdiction unless otherwise permitted by statute. None of the content in this book is a recommendation to buy, sell, or hold any financial product or an endorsement of any particular investment idea or strategy. None of the content in this book should be interpreted as investment advice. You are fully responsible for your investment decisions and should base these decisions on a wide variety of research and education, as well as your personal investment goals and risk tolerance.

*To my wife, Mary Kathryn, who helped me learn so many
of the concepts taught in this book and who supported
me every step of the way in the writing process.*

*To all of the couples I've had the privilege of
coaching through the material in this book, whose
progress inspires me each and every day.*

*And to Mr. Ray Greenwood, my 9th grade English teacher,
who taught this math nerd the power of a good story.*

Contents

"I'm Embarrassed to Tell Her About It..."

March 24th, 2017, was the day I learned that financial planning had almost nothing to do with math.

From my earliest memories of going to school as a child, I was always the math nerd in the class. I was the kid who would practice his multiplication tables for fun on the weekends in elementary school. The kid whose favorite high school class was trigonometry. The kid who took Linear Algebra as a senior in college because he had a free slot open on his schedule and "it might be a useful thing to know someday." (It wasn't.)

So, it probably shouldn't surprise anyone to learn that I became a financial planner—I thought it was a great career choice for a math nerd. I was ready to hit the ground running analyzing investment returns and doing time value of money calculations when I became a financial advisor in 2015. Armed with my spreadsheets and financial calculator, I was ready to change the lives of the people I worked with.

And until March 24th, 2017, I thought that was how it worked. I thought that all it took to answer a financial planning question was to solve the right math problem.

On that day in March, I had an introductory call scheduled with a man in his early thirties, who told me before our meeting that he was married with his first child on the way. (For the sake of confidentiality, let's call him "Doug.") When we opened the Zoom meeting (yes, Zoom was around back in 2017!), I was surprised to see that he was unaccompanied for our call. Up until this point, I had never had someone who was married show up to a financial planning call without their spouse present.

We started by going through the usual checklist of topics you'd probably expect to cover with a financial planner. I got the details about his credit card debt, student loans, the house he was hoping to buy in the next few months, and so on—but eventually, I decided that I had to address the elephant in the room.

"Out of curiosity, is there a reason why it's just you and me here today, and your wife isn't around?" I remember asking.

Doug paused, and I could tell he was hesitating. After a brief moment, he answered, "She had a work commitment and couldn't make it."

To this day, I don't remember *why* I got the sense he wasn't telling me the full story. "Okay," I replied. "Would you mind if I grabbed her email address so I can add her to our next meeting invite?"

He started shifting in his chair. "To tell you the truth, Bill," he said quietly after a moment, "she doesn't know about the credit card debt. And I'm embarrassed to tell her about it."

I knew right away that there wasn't a spreadsheet in the world that was going to be able to solve this particular problem. It hit me all at once: financial planning for couples wasn't *just* a math equation.

I knew I could help Doug clear up his credit card debt pretty quickly. But I also knew that if I were going to *really* help Doug use his money to create a life that he loved, we would need to dig deeper into how he and his wife managed money together.

That one meeting in March 2017 opened the floodgates. All of a sudden, I started seeing how emotions around money affected the way that the couples I met with were managing their finances together. A small sampling of these cases includes:

- The wife who told me in late 2017 that she wanted to work with a financial planner because, as she put it, "my husband isn't as financially savvy as he thinks he is."

- The couple who reached out to me because the stress and strain of living paycheck to paycheck were bleeding over to other areas of their relationship.

- The husband who called his wife "incredibly selfish" for wanting to change jobs and take a 20% pay cut so she could work fewer hours and spend more time at home in the evenings with their children.

- The woman who was putting off proposing to her long-time partner until she could get her debt under control so that, in her words, "I'm not burdening my partner with my horrible credit score."

- The engaged couple whose primary financial goal was to stop fighting about money and "make our finances less of a touchy subject."

- The dozen or so couples I've heard from where one spouse brought five figures worth of student loan debt into the marriage, and either a) the spouse with the student loans felt guilty for burdening their spouse with their debt, or b) the spouse without the student loans felt resentful toward the debt they "inherited" when they got married.

- The woman who was looking for a way to declare bankruptcy, even though her spouse had a six-figure income, because they had refused to combine any of their finances, and as a result, she was struggling to pay her bills.

Each of these couples came to me with financial questions they wanted answered. But the reality is that for each of them, the roadblocks in their way weren't financial. In truth, they were dealing with relationship and communication roadblocks.

I realized that if they could just learn how to talk about money in a more constructive way and learn to manage their finances in ways that worked with their unique money habits, values, and attitudes, they would make progress in both their financial lives and in their relationships.

MONEY AND MARRIAGE: LOST CAUSE OR GOLDEN OPPORTUNITY?

When examining the relationship between money and marriage, it only takes a quick Google search to understand the current state of affairs in the world of love and money.

In a nutshell: it's not good.

- A TD Bank study in 2019 found that 40% of millennial couples argue about money at least once a week.

- The same TD Bank study found that 29% of divorced Baby Boomers and 41% of divorced Gen Xers ended their marriages due to financial disagreements.

- A study by Ally Bank in 2018 found that money was the topic that caused the most stress for couples.

- A landmark study in the Family Relationships Journal in 2012 found that financial disagreements are the number one indicator of a future divorce.

The cause of these financial arguments ranges from day-to-day spending decisions to arguments about big financial goals to arguments about career and work/life balance. Wherever you turn, the data on money and marriage is grim. Money isn't only something that can break couples apart; it is one of the *most common reasons* that marriages fail.

It's easy to look at the research about how money impacts marriages and start drawing false conclusions. "If money is something that so many couples fight about, maybe it's best if we don't talk about it at all." "If managing money together causes couples to fight about money, maybe it's easiest if we stick to what we know and keep our finances separate." Not a week goes by when I don't meet a couple who fervently believes at least one of those two claims.

But after years of hearing stories like Doug's, reflecting on my own personal experience with the intersection of money and marriage, and having discussions with struggling couples, I came up with a theory. And I would go on to put this theory to the test, not just with Doug and his wife, but with countless couples across the country.

The theory was this: so much of the way we talk about the role that money plays in marriage focuses on the negative, but the opposite is true, too. When couples learn to manage their money well together, it doesn't just improve their financial status. It also makes their marriage stronger.

INTRODUCING: MARRIAGE-CENTERED FINANCIAL PLANNING

From my very first interaction with Doug back in 2017, I saw a unique opportunity to help couples accelerate their financial progress in a way that was uniquely suited to their relationship, and I started to approach these issues in a way that would make their marriage stronger.

In the intervening years, I developed and fine-tuned the process of *Marriage-Centered Financial Planning* outlined in this book. I've seen firsthand the power these concepts have had in the lives of couples across the country, and I'm excited to share them with you in this book.

In Part 1, I'll show you exactly what Marriage-Centered Financial Planning is, how it differs from traditional financial planning and marital advice, and the underlying concepts and principles you need to know in order to effectively implement a Marriage-Centered Financial Plan for your family. I'll also show you the fastest and easiest way to start making progress on your plan.

Then, we will work on building a solid foundation in the way you and your spouse approach money together in Part 2. I'll show you how to get your spouse on board with making financial changes, how to understand your spouse's money history and fundamental beliefs that drive the way they make financial decisions, and how to handle your financial differences to help you move forward financially as a family. We will also discuss some more extreme cases and the warning signs you should be aware of indicating the need to seek additional help.

Finally, in Part 3, you'll learn the step-by-step framework for creating a Marriage-Centered Financial Plan. We'll walk through the process from beginning to end, so you'll know the exact steps to take with your spouse to improve the way you manage and communicate about money together as a family.

This book is for you and your partner if:

- You're ready to go from feeling unsure, ashamed, or stressed to feeling confident and empowered about your family's finances.

- You're engaged or newly married and want to *prepare* to manage money effectively together as a new family to avoid problems down the road.

- You frequently argue about money with your spouse (or even worse, you avoid talking about money at all costs because you know that doing so will lead to money fights) and are ready to *repair* any damage that finances have done to your relationship.

- You're ready to have a clearly defined plan for achieving your most important dreams and goals as a couple to create the lives you love—together.

The processes and principles in this book have improved the financial trajectories of countless couples I've worked with over the years.

Marriage-Centered Financial Planning is the key to blending the traditional "math" component of financial planning with the deeper connection you desire with your spouse. By learning how to manage money effectively as a team with respect to your unique money habits, attitudes, and values, you won't just transform your financial state—you'll improve your marriage as well.

PART I

GETTING STARTED

CHAPTER 1

Defining Marriage-Centered Financial Planning

have to admit that when we hired you to be our financial planner, I really didn't expect you would basically become our financial therapist. It's kind of nice!"

I wasn't anticipating my second meeting with Rebecca and Robert to end on that particular note, but there we were. Two meetings in with a client, and I (apparently) had morphed from their "financial planner" to their "financial therapist."[1]

This was back in mid-2017—back around the time I was just beginning to realize that financial planning wasn't just about crunching numbers and making pretty spreadsheets. I don't remember exactly what prompted Rebecca to make this statement, and I definitely didn't expect it to become one of the pivotal moments of my career. To the best of my recollection, it came from a discussion we had about what she and her husband really wanted their money to be doing for them in their lives (this is something I'll teach you in Chapter 9).

What I *do* remember is that this was the first of many similar statements I heard from the couples I worked with in the following

---

1. To be clear: I am a financial planner with a LOT of experience helping couples get on the same financial page, but I am not a mental health professional. And while I have since become a Certified Financial Therapist-Level I™ Practitioner, that was *not* the case back in 2017!

months. I hadn't yet figured out *why* my clients were suddenly referring to me as a "financial counselor" or a "financial therapist," but it quickly got to the point where it was happening more often than not.

I can't stress this enough—my journey down the path of becoming a Marriage-Centered Financial Planner was not an intentional one. I started down this road by accident. I decided to launch Pacesetter Planning back in 2016 to work with engaged and newlywed couples only because I was newly married myself. (Note: having quit my job, gotten married, and started a business within a three-month stretch, I don't necessarily advocate trying to do all of these things at once!)

It wasn't until the fourth or fifth time I heard a client refer to me as a "financial therapist" that I decided to explore what that really meant and why I was hearing it so frequently.

At the time, I was working with a business coach who *strongly* pushed me to focus my work on couples' dynamics with money when I told him about the feedback I was getting from clients. "Nobody is doing that type of work effectively right now," he told me. "You should really lean into that and be *the* financial planner for couples who are fighting about money."

And yet, I hesitated.

It wasn't that I disagreed with my coach's conclusion. I clearly saw the need and could tell that I had some skill in helping couples work through these disputes in the nascent financial planning process I was using at the time.

But back in late 2017 and early 2018, I felt like a fraud.

It wasn't just that my process for helping couples get on the same financial page and use their money to make their marriages stronger was still in the early stages of development.

It was because I was having some of these disputes in my *own* marriage. How could I be *the* money and marriage financial planner when I was struggling with these things in my own life?

My wife, Mary Kathryn, and I started dating back in 2007 when I had just turned eighteen. To help frame how long ago that was, when we first started dating, people were doing the Soulja Boy (non-iron-ically). One of our first dates was to see the movie *Juno* in the theaters. It was a long time ago, to put it mildly!

We dated through college, and she enrolled in med school right after we graduated. I had a very comfortable job doing financial consulting at a Big Four accounting firm in DC. She was in med school, and in early 2015, we had a few big decisions to make as she finished school and started her residency training.

To say that we were ill-equipped to make those decisions is an understatement.

We were trying to balance a *lot* of things, and we just didn't know how to do it:

Career decisions: The best places for her to get her training were in different places across the country—not where I was working and living. Meanwhile, I was just starting to hit my stride in my career. And while, in hindsight, there were some clear signs that the job was burning me out and wasn't the right long-term fit for me, trying to figure out the *timing* of when I'd leave was difficult.

Location: Should we move to a place where one of us was already living, should we try something new as an adventure for a few years, or should we move to be closer to one of our families on opposite sides of the country?

Income and work/life balance decisions: Leaving my job would almost definitely mean either taking a pay cut or traveling for work five days of the week, every week, year-round. Were *those* the right decisions for us to make for our family?

We were trying to weigh a ton of different factors against each other and had no proverbial "north star" to guide us. On the one hand, we were ready to merge households, get engaged, and start making financial decisions together. On the other hand, we didn't really know how to do that—trying to balance factors relating to each of our jobs, our homes, our families, and our workload. We hadn't taken the time or we just didn't know how to identify what was most important to us as a family. This made it very hard to be flexible and meet each other to reach a consensus.

Without having any success criteria, we didn't know how to make a decision of this magnitude together … but we had to do something.

So, we made the one choice that's never made sense for anyone, anywhere to make: we decided to move to Philadelphia. (My apologies to my Philadelphia readers—let's just say it didn't work out between Philadelphia and me.)

There was plenty of good that happened during those years. We got engaged and then got married. But behind the scenes, our decision-making regarding those same topics— financial decisions, location, career decisions—well, we still weren't much better at that.

And so, these problems lingered below the surface for a few years until it was time to decide our next move at the conclusion of her residency training. I'll spare you the details, but let's just say that we still didn't know how to guide our decision-making as a family. So, the underlying challenges we had relating to communication and making decisions together quickly boiled to the surface—right around the time I was starting to learn how to help other couples get on the same financial page.

I knew what I wanted; it was the same thing the couples I worked with wanted in their work with a "financial therapist." I wanted not just confidence in the financial decisions we were making but also to have those financial decisions be an asset to my marriage rather than a liability.

I knew I didn't have all the answers to some of the marriage and money questions my clients posed to me or the questions I had in my own marriage. But at the same time, I was starting to see my clients get some major results.

It was almost like completing the early stages of a jigsaw puzzle. I had all the pieces out in front of me, I had a clear picture of what the end result should look like, and I was trying to put all the pieces of this process together in the most efficient way.

All the while, I was getting great feedback on the money and marriage work I was doing publicly.

Upon presenting a very early version of the Marriage-Centered Financial Planning process at a mastermind group, I'll never forget how quiet the room got after I finished talking through the process. No applause, no questions, nothing. Admittedly, I wasn't sure if this was a good thing or not until one of the women in the front row quietly stated, "This work is going to save marriages."

I knew then that I was onto something big, even if I still wasn't confident enough to declare the process ready for "prime time."

Shortly thereafter, I got a personalized message from one of the leaders in the money and relationships space in response to a LinkedIn post that I made, commending the content I was creating and emphasizing the power it had to change marriages. (I wish I saved a copy of the video, but it's one of those things that I'll never forget.)

A little while later, I had a financial planner reach out to me to hire me as *their* financial planner to help her and her husband figure out a way to manage money that worked well for both of their individual money habits and values. You might not expect a financial planner to want to hire their own financial planner. But she saw the value in my process to help not just their bottom line but their family as well.

All the signs were there; I just wasn't ready on a personal level.

It wasn't until my wife and I moved forward that I finally connected all the dots.

Ultimately, I realized that I wasn't a fraud for having money and marriage struggles in my own personal life while I was helping my clients work through similar issues—I was just still trying to figure out the right process to follow. And soon, I discovered that having these sorts of challenges in my own life didn't make me a hypocrite or a bad financial planner.

Instead, it helped me put myself in my clients' shoes, to understand what they were going through, and it helped me speed up the journey to finding the right solution for them.

My own struggles with balancing the tradeoffs of different financial decisions ultimately accelerated my path of designing a planning process specifically built around these types of decisions that could work for any couple, regardless of the specific relationship dynamics at play. And while a marriage counselor was able to help my wife and I unpack these issues, make new decisions, and move forward as a family, working with one also showed me the challenges traditional marriage counseling has when dealing with financial questions.

Once I had found the path forward in my own marriage, I dove headfirst into testing my theories and processes. I integrated my approach not just with best practices in the financial planning world but also with the work of leading relationship experts and researchers in the Financial Therapy Association.

By blending the experiences in my own marriage and the questions and issues I saw facing the couples I worked with, I identified the gaps in the way both financial planners and relationship counselors handled money and marriage issues, did the research, and developed the Marriage-Centered Financial Planning process that has helped countless couples across the country over the past few years.

Whether you are looking to *prepare* your family for potential money and marriage pitfalls down the road, or if you're looking to *repair* your relationship from financial disputes you've had in the past, Marriage-Centered Financial Planning is the right vehicle for you to make the changes you desire.

IT'S NOT YOUR FAULT

If you're struggling with finding the right approach to financial decisions in your marriage, here's the most important thing you need to understand right out of the gate: it's not your fault.

Nobody ever taught us how to manage money *on our own*, never mind how to make financial decisions with someone else. Most of us never learned about personal finance when we were in school. We might have learned about trigonometry, the Holy Roman Empire, and how to play the recorder—which I'm sure are skills all of you are putting to good use right now—but we didn't learn how to manage and invest money. And unless your education curriculum looked very different from mine, we certainly didn't learn how to be a good spouse in school, either!

This means if you're looking to get on the same financial page as your spouse and use your money to make your marriage stronger, you likely have turned to other resources in the past to solve these problems before you came across this book. And on both the "money" and "marriage" sides of the coin, the current landscape leaves a lot to be desired.

On the financial side, there are a few big problems with how personal finance "experts" talk about money and marriage:

Personal finance experts tend to give one-size-fits-all advice that ignores the specific differences you have with your spouse. You can find money gurus out there who will tell you that you always need to combine 100% of your finances after you get married, and you can find equally respected gurus who will tell you never to combine any of your money with your spouse. Aside from creating a lot of unnecessary confusion, there are a few problems with this dichotomy:

- Both of those options can be problematic for your marriage, depending on the circumstances. "You should always combine 100% of your bank accounts, always" sounds good in theory … but if you and your spouse have a few specific differences in financial habits, this one step could very easily make your financial arguments *worse* (as we will discuss in Chapter 11). And you probably don't need me to tell you that, on the flip side, never combining any of your money can create some logistical barriers to getting on the same financial page.

- It's very hard to find moderated guidance that actually looks at the specific issues you and your spouse are having and has a nuanced discussion about the right solution to fit your needs. In today's soundbite and social media influencer-based world, so many of our discussions get reduced to one-size-fits-all advice that avoids the type of nuance that is so critical to money and marriage decisions. You could theoretically find a good financial planner to help you do this, but that leads us to the second big problem with how financial professionals talk about marriage and money issues …

Most financial planners treat couples' dynamics around money as "third rail" issues to be avoided at all costs. I certainly wasn't alone in the industry in my early days in thinking that the proper role of a financial planner was to handle issues that show up in the spreadsheets rather than between the bedsheets. I actually received formal financial training that told me to immediately pause a conversation with a client whenever a couple started bickering about money and refer them to a marriage counselor.

From discussions at conferences to posts on message boards and everything in between, there have been at least half a dozen times I've personally witnessed good financial planners express exasperation, frustration, or even contempt about the inability of their married clients to get on the same financial page. It's very common in my industry to take these conflicts as an inevitability rather than something that can be solved. These financial planners are *very* good at the mathematical side of financial planning. But most would rather avoid dealing with financial conflict and stick to the spreadsheets.

And at worst, financial planners can exacerbate these issues or fall into gender-based stereotypes that, to put it delicately, don't help the problem at all. I've had multiple women tell me they've met with people in my industry who would only direct the conversation and decision-making questions to their husband rather than to both of them. Yikes.

So, if financial experts don't give guidance that's appropriately tailored to couples and don't want to handle marital differences around money, the natural assumption might be that couples dealing with these issues would be better suited by working with a marriage counselor.

However, in my experience, I've found that marriage counselors aren't always a ton of help with financial questions:

Marriage counseling tends to handle backward-looking issues better than forward-looking decisions. If you have a history of trauma, a counselor is absolutely the right person to help you work through these issues. Therapy (whether individual or couples) plays a critical role in helping you heal and move forward, and this certainly includes issues related to financial trauma.

But the problem that happens too often in working with marriage counselors (as I found in my own experience) is that it gets very easy to stay focused on the past. Working with a counselor plays an important role, but too often, it leads couples to do the equivalent of driving a car and only looking in the rearview mirror rather than looking at the road ahead.

Marriage counseling is great in the sense that it helps you learn how to communicate and work through trauma. But the problem is that often, it's very *backward* looking. Therapy is constantly going backward to find solutions to problems, which can be effective—and is often necessary—but is usually not sufficient. I've found that constantly pulling backward is also a great way to get yourself stuck in the past. You need a north star that will give you something to work toward to help pull you forward.

And even if you find a marriage counselor who shares this sort of philosophy, a second issue tends to crop up related to how therapists talk about money.

Therapists aren't very good at handling financial discussions. I understand that this might sound like a bit of a stereotype at first, but study after study has shown that therapists, including marriage therapists, tend to be ill-equipped to help clients handle financial issues. Dr. Glen Gabbard, a psychiatrist at Baylor University, has described money as the "dirtiest topic in psychoanalysis. It is avoided in scientific papers [in therapeutic and psychiatry journals], clinical case conferences, and analytic seminars." In *Money Talks - in Therapy, Society,* *and Life*, the authors note at the outset that money has been termed the "last taboo" in the therapeutic realm, not just for patients but also for therapists.

THE RIGHT PATH FORWARD: MARRIAGE-CENTERED FINANCIAL PLANNING

So, if all of these other options are the *wrong* approach to help you and your spouse get and stay on the same financial page, what's involved in the *right* approach? I've introduced the concept of Marriage-Centered Financial Planning and talked about my journey to develop the process, but what does that actually *mean*?

Why do I consider Marriage-Centered Financial Planning not just a "better" financial plan but a completely different way to approach the way you make financial decisions as a family?

The long answer, of course, is detailed in the rest of this book, which will show you exactly how to implement these strategies in your own family. But let me give you an overview before we dive into the details:

It puts your marriage at the center of your financial decisions so that your money will make your marriage stronger. By realigning your focus to put your marriage at the center of your financial plan, you won't just make financial progress by implementing the plan. You'll make your marriage stronger, too.

Most people measure their financial progress by "only" looking at the bottom-line financial numbers. Marriage-Centered Financial Planning certainly doesn't *ignore* the financial metrics, but the primary measure of success is how aligned you and your spouse are when it comes to money. (We'll discuss the five key benchmarks we use to evaluate this in the next chapter.) If you and your spouse are working together and managing money in a way that makes your relationship stronger, financial success is inevitable.

Imagine you and your partner are riding in a sailboat. "Typical" financial planning views financial freedom as the destination of the boat ride—the distant shore you are sailing toward, with the goal of getting there as quickly as possible.

Done correctly, a Marriage-Centered Financial Plan treats your *dream life* as the destination, and your marriage is the boat ride you take to get there. It's not a race. There's no such thing as moving "too slow" or being "too far" from the shore you're trying to reach. We just want the boat ride to get you there safely and be as smooth as possible.

Money, in this context, isn't the destination or even the journey—it's the sail in the sailboat. It's just a tool you use to get there. You can improve how you use the sail to speed up the journey, but in a proper Marriage-Centered Financial Plan, money is just a tool in your toolkit.

It strikes the right balance between the "money" and "marriage" sides of the Money/Marriage Scale. I like to think of a family's financial plan as a giant metaphorical balance scale. On one side, we have the marital issues that often manifest as money disputes or difficult decisions. And on the other side, we have the data-driven financial situation of the family.

THE MONEY/MARRIAGE SCALE

To achieve long-term financial stability *and* long-term marital stability, you need to strike the right balance between both sides of this Money/Marriage Scale.

In most cases, couples will have a favorite "side" of the Money/Marriage Scale they like to focus on and one they feel less sure about. Maybe you and your spouse feel like you're in terrible financial condition but are completely in sync when it comes to financial decision-making and your attitudes about money. Or conversely, maybe you're in fantastic financial shape, but money is just something you don't talk about as a family.

The reality is that you constantly need to work on *both* the state of your finances and the way you manage money as a family. You need to find the right balance between the money and marriage sides of the scale, which could mean working on both equally or prioritizing the area you're the weakest in, depending on the circumstances. The good news is that the Marriage-Centered Financial Planning process will help you work on both—not just to fix any issues you and your partner are having now but also to prevent issues from arising down the road.

A runner can't just focus on running and ignore other aspects of their fitness for very long before creating bigger problems for themselves; without appropriate cross-training, core strengthening, and stretching, their progress will stagnate (or worse, they will injure themselves). Money and marriage work exactly the same way. Marriage-Centered Financial Planning helps you work on each side of the scale to maximize your long-term potential while reducing the risk of falling apart financially or in your relationship.

It helps you identify and tailor the "right" decisions to your specific money tendencies as a family. No two relationships (and no two financial situations) are exactly the same. The "right" choice for you as a family could very well be the wrong decision for others. It's critical, then, to appropriately tailor the way you manage money as a family to the specific dynamics of your relationship so that you make your marriage stronger in the process.

Physicians don't hand out prescriptions to patients without making a diagnosis first, and the same applies to making good money decisions for couples. By diagnosing what's wrong first, you will be able to quickly implement the right solution the first time, which will accelerate your progress.

It focuses on five guiding principles to help your decision-making. It might be easy to assume that "identifying and tailoring the *right* decisions to your specific money tendencies as a family" would leave things very open-ended for the purposes of this book. You might worry that tailoring financial decisions to your unique habits and values as a couple would provide you with an endless string of questions with no answers.

On the contrary, Marriage-Centered Financial Planning is a principles-based approach to help you and your spouse make the right financial decisions specifically customized for your family. There are five principles designed to be the focal point of what we measure in this process to help you make decisions to move forward financially and to evaluate your progress.

These five principles are so important that they deserve a deeper dive and are the subject of our next chapter.

MARRIAGE-CENTERED FINANCIAL PLANNING

Ultimately, Marriage-Centered Financial Planning isn't just an investment plan … it's an investment unto itself. By putting the time and energy into this opportunity for your family, you are investing in your family's future success—financial and otherwise.

This sort of investment might not show up on the balance sheet, but it's the most important type of investment your family can make.

CHAPTER 2

The Five Principles of Marriage-Centered Financial Planning

Back in the fall of 2018, I had a first meeting with a couple (let's call them Mark and Maria) who could only be described with one word: extreme. Not necessarily in a bad way, mind you, but as you'll see below, the "math" portion of their financial plan dealt with some pretty extreme numbers for a couple right out of grad school.

As we got further and further into the meeting, it seemed like *every single factor* about the couple's financial situation was extreme:

- Student loan debt of over $200,000, all in Mark's name.

- Income: nearly $350,000 between the two of them … but Maria was hoping to change careers and take a $100,000 pay cut in the process.

- They were getting ready to buy a $1.1 million house.

- They had a negative overall net worth that was quickly trending positive.

The good news for Mark and Maria was that they quickly had the opportunity to build a strong financial foundation for their family, giving them the flexibility and freedom they needed to accomplish their goals of buying a home and Maria's change of career. After building their financial plan, we agreed on a course of action:

- Both Maria and Mark agreed that they wanted to get rid of their student loans as soon as possible and that doing so would make it much easier for them to reduce their household income and eventually buy a home. We agreed that they would pay off the loans as soon as possible using a combination of their money in savings and everything they were saving on a month-to-month basis.

- They also agreed that Maria's work/life balance (or lack thereof) in her current job was holding their family back and that it would be worth the financial sacrifice to take a pay cut while pursuing a new opportunity.

- Finally, they agreed that while homeownership was important to both of them, they would feel much more confident pursuing such a big purchase if they were buying from a position of financial strength. They agreed on wanting to take care of the loans and the career change first and revisiting the house decision afterward.

They agreed to their course of action, and I sent them on their merry way to start paying off their debt. Mark, Maria, and I agreed to meet every three months to monitor their progress and adjust their plan as needed.

Eight days later, I met with a second couple (let's call them Paul and Peggy). Here's the interesting thing about Paul and Peggy: their financial situation was nearly a mirror image of that of Mark and Maria in several ways:

- Six-figure student loan debt.

- Very high household incomes, with a potential career change for Peggy on the horizon.

- Home purchase goal in an expensive real estate market.

- Negative net worth, with a *lot* of potential to grow quickly in the coming years.

As a result, the recommendations I gave to Paul and Peggy were very much in line with what I told Mark and Maria: pay down the student loans as quickly as possible, work on finding the next job, and save for a house after stabilizing their family's financial foundation. Just like their predecessors, Peggy and Paul agreed to the game plan and told me they'd see me again in three months.

Truth be told, I kind of forgot how similar the two couples were in the intervening months. But because they were on the same meeting schedule, I ended up having meetings with Mark/Maria and Peggy/Paul within a few days of each other three months after I gave them their initial financial plan.

What I discovered during those meetings was *not* what I was expecting.

Once again, I met with Mark and Maria first. And I could tell just from the look on Maria's face when she joined the meeting that they had some good news to share.

"We've paid off nearly $75,000 in student loan debt over the past three months!" Maria proudly exclaimed, almost before I had finished asking how things were going. "And I have a few leads on some jobs that could be *amazing!*"

They were doing great. They were working together, they knew the exact steps they should take, and they were executing on their plan flawlessly. We agreed to meet in another three months.

Mark and Maria set such a high bar that I eagerly anticipated the next meeting with Peggy and Paul. If Mark and Maria made such good progress, then surely, I could expect a similar story from a couple in an identical financial situation, right?

Wrong.

The good news was that Peggy and Paul were still making the minimum payments on their loans, and they had reduced the total balance by a few thousand dollars. The bad news was that they hadn't used *any* of the extra money they had in savings to pay down the balance of the loans, and they didn't make *any* extra monthly payments on the loans to chip away at the balance as they had agreed to.

Careful not to scold them for not following through on their plan, I thought for a minute before asking them, "What do you think is standing in your way from starting to pay down the loans?"

They came up with a list of questions that were indicative of what was holding them back:

- "Should we really be focusing on paying down the private student loans instead of the federal student loans? Which loan should we pay down first?"

- "How much money should we be paying on the loans each month?"

- "Should we be using both of our money to pay down the loans, or should we only pay for our individual loans and let our spouse handle the rest?"

- "How often should we be reviewing our loan paydown progress together?"

- "How do we make sure to follow through on the plan?"

We came up with answers to these questions. They agreed on the next step (to pay off the smallest private loan in full, right away), and we agreed to meet three months later.

And once again, over a ten-day time period, three months later, the process repeated itself. Mark and Maria made a *ton* of progress on their loans. And while Peggy and Paul had made some improvements and were starting to chip away at the loan balance, their progress on their debt payoff goal was much slower than I knew it could be.

This continued over the course of a few more meetings. And it ended with Maria and Mark paying off their loans in full, while taking a pay cut, in the same amount of time it took Peggy and Paul to pay off just over one-third of their loans.

Seeing this case study play out in real time made me wonder: what were the factors causing Mark and Maria to have such outstanding financial success? And what factors were holding Peggy and Paul back?

The obstacles clearly weren't financial, and they *definitely* weren't related to the underlying money math. Like I said, their financial situations were nearly identical, so on paper, you'd expect their progress to be the same.

Something else was clearly at play here. And I was determined to figure out what it was so I could better help couples handle these dynamics going forward.

THE FIVE PRINCIPLES OF MARRIAGE-CENTERED FINANCIAL PLANNING

What keeps couples from making financial progress? The financial obstacles that hold people back are a big part of this. Whether it be a lack of income, a lot of debt, or anything in between, there are sometimes clear and tangible financial roadblocks that can hinder progress.

But more often than not, there are intangible factors that are the root of the problem. These factors aren't necessarily financial in nature but very clearly hold people back from financial success.

After reviewing Mark and Maria's case against Peggy and Paul's and then examining the patterns I've seen hold couples back over the years, I realized there are only a few specific types of emotional or behavior-based roadblocks couples need to address on their journey to financial success. Specifically, there are five key drivers of financial planning success for couples to make both their finances and their marriages stronger.

I call these five drivers the Five Principles of Marriage-Centered Financial Planning. These five principles are the keys to help propel you and your spouse forward on *both* sides of the Money/Marriage Scale.

The Five Principles are **Confidence, Coordination, Communication, Clarity,** and **Commitment.**

Here's the interesting thing about these principles: they apply

THE FIVE PRINCIPLES OF MARRIAGE-CENTERED FINANCIAL PLANNING

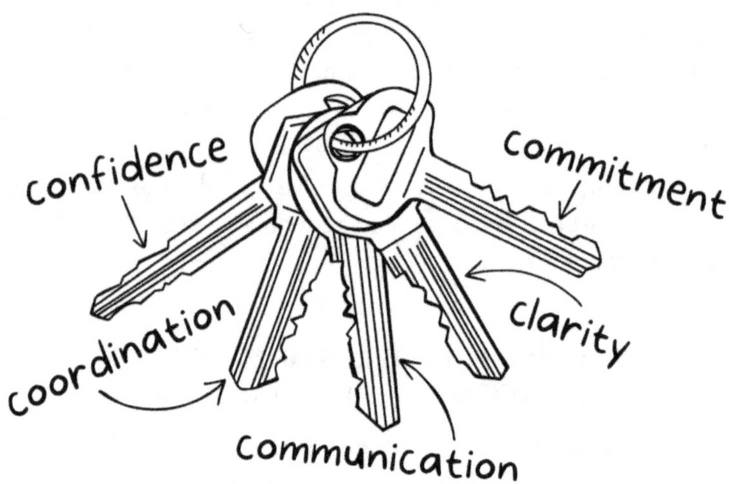

regardless of what sort of financial shape you're in. Whether you have hundreds of thousands of dollars of debt or you are millionaires, these Five Principles of Marriage-Centered Financial Planning are the key to helping you and your spouse manage money more effectively together.

Some of the principles are more likely to create challenges for you at different stages of your personal finance journey. But they're all important, all the time. It's critical to continually work on improving your standing with each of these principles.

The rest of this chapter will provide an overview of each of the five principles, and every subsequent chapter will give you some specific strategies and tactics to use to improve the way you and your spouse utilize them. We won't literally touch on every single principle in every single chapter, but by the time you reach the end of this book, you'll have a roadmap full of ways to work on all five principles in your marriage.

As we walk through the overview of each of the five principles below, I encourage you to reflect on each of them and what role they play in the way you and your spouse manage money together. By better understanding your starting point with each of the five principles, you'll gain an even bigger appreciation of how far you'll go on your journey through the rest of this book.

By the way, it's very common for you to be much better at one or two of these principles than the others. By focusing on the areas where you and your spouse are relatively weak, you'll be able to quickly strengthen your marriage by focusing on the low-hanging fruit.

Confidence

Having talked to hundreds of people about the state of their finances over the years, I've found the three most common feelings people have about money are:

- Anxiety
- Guilt
- Stress

Unfortunately, these feelings tend to be self-fulfilling. The anxiety, stress, or guilt that so many of us feel about the state of our finances tends to either cause us to avoid dealing with our money altogether, or paralyzes us and stops us from taking action to fix the problem. And when you're personally feeling this stress and strain, your marriage will feel it, too.

When you're under this sort of stress because of your finances (or anything else, for that matter), it weighs you down. It makes it harder for you to connect effectively with your spouse.

Financial stress impacts the way you and your spouse spend time together. It impacts the way you talk to each other. It impacts the things you're able to do with your spouse. It affects the food you choose to buy, the activities you complete together, and the amount of time you're able to spend together.

I've been there myself. Back when I left my job in 2016 to start my company, a month after we got married, my income went down to zero. Two years earlier, I had been working for a Big Four accounting firm. I went from having a great salary and benefits to having no income until I could build my client base.

This decision was one that has paid off… but I still remember how hard it was to get the business off the ground back in 2016. Working around the clock, every day of the week, with no base income was a *huge* source of financial stress. I knew that things would get better, but my short-term confidence was shot due to the financial stress of having no income.

The financial stress of trying to get a business off the ground was *brutal*. There was a lot of pressure on me to get my income up, and it *absolutely* bled into our relationship. As I shared in Chapter 1, a few things were going on behind the scenes that contributed to the relationship challenges we had in our first year of marriage, but financial stress was *definitely* a part of this.

The antidote to this sort of financial stress or anxiety isn't necessarily easy to implement, but the good news is that it's easy to identify. The way to move past financial stress and anxiety is to build your financial *confidence*.

It's no coincidence that the strength of our marriage rebounded as my income started to grow and our financial confidence increased. Improving our confidence in our financial situation didn't save our marriage on its own, but removing the financial stress definitely helped us grow stronger together.

Building your financial confidence is one of the most important steps you can take as a family when it comes to money. Even if you don't literally improve your financial bottom line right away, having a financial confidence boost will give you the strength you need to move forward.

I intentionally list confidence as the first principle of Marriage-Centered Financial Planning because it is the principle that holds the most people back from using their money to create the lives they love. Even if you are flawlessly executing on the other principles, a lack of confidence in your ability to handle money as a family will hold you back from achieving your goals.

The key to building your family's financial confidence is to have a clear, step-by-step plan to follow. When you know the exact steps you need to take to achieve your financial goals—and you start executing on the plan by focusing on one thing at a time—you might be surprised at how quickly your financial guilt, shame, stress, and anxiety transform into financial confidence and empowerment.

Coordination

It's almost impossible for couples to make sustained financial progress without working together. If you and your spouse are on different wavelengths when it comes to money, you will inadvertently undermine each other's progress and hold yourselves back through a lack of financial coordination.

It's hard to learn how to manage money effectively with another person, even if it's the person you're closest to. But learning how to be coordinated in the way you manage money with your spouse is one of the most important steps you can take to solidifying the strength of your marriage.

It's worth noting that I'm not necessarily talking about combining bank accounts in this discussion; we will revisit that decision in Chapter 11. You don't need to literally combine every single penny you have to improve your financial coordination with your spouse.

Instead, you want to improve the way you coordinate making big financial decisions together and, in turn, how you allocate your money to support those decisions.

Until you get married, you can generally make big decisions and allocate your financial resources by yourself. When you're single, the only things that matter in big decisions are *your* life, *your* career, *your* money, *your* home, and so on. All you need to do is evaluate your financial resources and priorities when making a big decision.

When you get married, that needs to change. You shift from thinking about "me" to thinking about "we." This isn't limited to financial decisions, of course, but it definitely includes your money.

It's very normal to have different attitudes and perspectives when it comes to finances (we're going to talk at length about specific strategies to use to handle these differences in Part 2). But making the shift to being coordinated in the way you manage money with your spouse is a *critical* step to take.

I know a lot of couples who have really struggled to shift from making financial decisions based on their own priorities to making financial decisions based on their new family's priorities. Mary Kathryn and I also struggled with this, as I previously shared.

When you get on the same page and start working together to dream about your future, you deepen the strength of your relationship, *and* you also start to naturally watch your bank accounts grow over time to reach these goals and dreams.

When you're able to make this shift, it's a *really* unifying thing for your family.

When you start shifting your thinking from your own priorities to your family's priorities and learn how to do this when it comes to your money, this will naturally make your relationship stronger. What you're actually doing is learning how to prioritize your marriage rather than yourself with how you are using your financial resources.

This is a transition all couples need to learn how to make, and it is easier for some people than others. But by doing this with your money and thinking of your money as "our" money to be allocated to "our" goals, your marriage *will* become stronger in the process.

Even if you decide to keep some of your money separate after you get married, it's impossible to avoid the fact that most of you and your spouse's income and other financial resources will be directed toward your shared family expenses and goals. This will happen naturally over time.

By focusing on your family's most important goals, working together to achieve them, and learning the most optimal way for you and your spouse to manage money together, your thinking will shift, helping you to be more unified.

Communication

This is probably the least surprising of the five principles. (If you haven't heard that communication is one of the keys to a strong marriage, I don't know what to tell you.) But even though it's something that everybody knows in theory, it's often the hardest for couples to implement together in practice.

The problems are twofold. First and foremost, communication, in general, is one of those things you're never done "fixing" in a marriage. It's something you need to work at and improve on continually.

Secondly, talking about money is particularly challenging for most people. In many ways, money is the last remaining taboo in our society.

Case in point: a study conducted by University College London a few years ago surveyed 15,000 men and women in Great Britain and found that people are *seven times* more likely to tell a stranger details about their sex life than they are to tell a stranger their salary.

Back in the day, there were four topics you were always supposed to avoid talking about in polite company—politics, religion, sex, and money. You've probably talked about the first three with your partner already (and if you *haven't* talked about any of these things with your partner, you probably should soon!). It's also time to add "money" to the list.

Nobody *likes* to talk about money. But if we could get just a little more comfortable talking about it, we'd be a *lot* better off. And that certainly includes the way you talk about money with your spouse.

It is impossible to competently manage money with another person without effective communication. Most of us aren't naturally good at talking about money; it's something we need to work at and practice over time.

But by improving the way you listen to your spouse about the topic of money and communicate your own financial needs and wants with your spouse, your communication across the board will improve. By learning to manage money effectively with your partner, and the inevitable communication it involves, you're taking one of the most important steps to improve your relationship by working on your communication skills.

If money is something you and your spouse fight about, improving the way you communicate with each other about money will remove one of the biggest challenges and pain points in your marriage.

If money *isn't* something you and your spouse fight about,

improving the way you communicate with each other about money will make a good marriage great.

Clarity

Before we talk about how to improve the state of your finances with your partner, it's worth asking: how clear are you on your financial status as a couple *today*?

None of us start our marriage with a blank financial slate. We come into the marriage with old bank accounts, retirement accounts, and/or debts. Unless you are proactive in implementing a system to manage all of these separate accounts as a household (at the same time you're opening new ones), it's very easy to lose sight of where your money is today and where it's going.

One of the biggest things that can hold couples back is a lack of clarity about the state of their finances as a couple. On one end of the spectrum, this could mean having so many accounts that you have a hard time keeping track of them all. On the other end, it could involve intentionally hiding accounts or debts from your spouse.

Whether it involves losing track of old individual accounts or hiding credit cards, one of the quickest ways to sow distrust in your marriage is to not be open and transparent with your spouse.

Learning to manage your money effectively with your spouse will necessitate that you put all of your chips on the table—the good, the bad, and the ugly—and have a system in place to manage them with clarity for your family. Regardless of the past financial mistakes of you or your partner, being honest and clear about your financial state will help you work together and build a better future.

Once again, "clarity" doesn't necessarily mean "combining accounts." But it *does* involve not hiding anything *and* having a system in place to easily keep track of everything. Every aspect of your financial lives should be out in the open and easy to find.

And when you make yourself vulnerable in this way, you're naturally going to come out on the other side much closer to your spouse.

In Chapter 8, we're going to talk in more detail about the concept of financial infidelity and how not being transparent about the state of your finances can break your marriage. But for now, understand that the opposite is true, too. By being completely and openly clear about the state of your finances, you can increase the trust and strength of your marriage.

Commitment

The first financial plan I wrote was over forty pages long. I was quite proud of it. It answered every single question the client could come up with, walked them through various scenarios, and contained about twenty different graphs. From the technical side, it was a bulletproof financial plan.

When I gave it to the client, they said it was exactly what they needed, and we agreed to meet again to review their progress in a month. Everything was perfect—or so I thought.

When the client came to that meeting a month later, I was surprised to see they had made *zero* progress in implementing their financial plan. They hadn't completed a single action item. Not one.

That long financial plan was "good" in the sense that it addressed everything it needed to address, but it was utterly ineffectual in its most important job—guiding the client toward their future dreams. It was so complicated that the client couldn't follow it. It tried to do so many things that the client didn't know what to focus on. It might have answered their questions, but it did nothing to inspire them to take action. And, as a result, the plan didn't get implemented, and the client didn't make the progress they wanted.

The principle of commitment is all about the follow-through. It's about doing the things you say are most important to you. It's about acting on the plans you set for yourself.

Two of the most common areas I see couples struggling with committing to their financial plans relate to life insurance and their estate planning documents.

Once you get married, and especially once you have kids, everybody knows they need to have a will and adequate term life insurance in place to support their family if something were to happen to them. But very, very few people actually do it.

I often find that executing wills and applying for life insurance are the very last financial planning recommendations that clients follow through on. We know that they are important, but we don't actually make them a priority.

Unless of course, you know someone who died without a will or life insurance, and you have been able to see firsthand the impact this can have on a family. In my experience, couples who have seen others live through these consequences are much quicker at getting their own insurance coverage implemented.

At the end of the day, a financial plan is nothing without the follow-through. By focusing on increasing commitment to making financial progress, you and your spouse will accelerate your family's results.

If you're struggling with following through with your best financial intentions, you should consider narrowing down the number of things you're trying to do at once to feel less overwhelmed. You should also literally put time on your calendar to give yourself time to focus on finances, and set smaller goals with relatively short deadlines. (There's a reason that nobody ever sticks to their New Year's Resolutions—a year is far too long a timeframe to set for your goals.)

Narrow the scope of what you're committing to and shorten the timeframe, and you might be surprised at how your financial progress accelerates.

The action steps you follow should be easy to understand, in line with what's most important to you as a family, and the next step should be very clearly laid out for you. If you try to bite off more than you can chew all at once, you'll fail.

———

No amount of good financial management is going to save a broken marriage. A marriage can't survive on good financial habits alone.

But, by improving the way you and your spouse handle each of the Five Principles of Marriage-Centered Financial Planning, you won't just improve the way you manage money with your spouse, but you can also make your marriage stronger in the process.

Importantly, this only has a little to do with the dollars and cents involved. Literally improving your financial situation can help your marriage, but the real benefits come from the results of you working together on such an intimate subject.

Now that you understand the Five Principles, it's time to revisit a more specific version of the Marriage-Centered Financial Planning graphic from the previous chapter.

MARRIAGE-CENTERED FINANCIAL PLANNING

The five principles of confidence, clarity, communication, coordination, and commitment are the "wind in your sails" on your journey. The better you and your spouse get at living each of these five principles in your marriage, the faster your financial progress will be.

CHAPTER 3

Getting Your "Quick Win"

Sarah and Sam were unsure about pretty much everything. When I first met them back in 2018, they were perpetually stuck on just about every aspect of their finances.

They couldn't decide how much to put into their retirement accounts. They disagreed about how much money to put into Sarah's small business. They had vastly different priorities when it came to the importance of getting their estate plan and life insurance done. They had different philosophies when it came to picking investments. They were torn about where their next house should be located and when they should plan to buy.

Just about every aspect of Sam and Sarah's finances was stagnated, and it was taking a toll on their relationship.

The only thing they could agree on—and I mean the *only* thing—was that their car loan needed to be gone.

It came up in our initial conversation almost as an afterthought—a four-year-old car loan with a balance of just over $3,000. At their current payment amount, it would be paid off in about a year, but both Sam and Sarah wanted it paid off and out of their lives *now*.

"So, it sounds like it's time to just pay off the car loan," I said matter-of-factly.

Sarah and Sam responded with a quiet silence.

"What do you mean we should just pay it off now? It's only $3,000, and it's not like we can't afford the payments. Shouldn't we put the money toward something else?" Sam asked after a few moments.

"No, you should pay off the car loan," I explained. "In fact, we should log into your account and pay it off before we get off the call.

"You both said that the car loan is weighing on you—even if you don't think it *should* be a big deal, it clearly is something that's on both of your minds.

"Even more importantly, it's something you both *agree* that you want to get rid of. You've got plenty of money sitting in your checking account. Even after you pay the loans off, you'll still be able to make some retirement account contributions or put money into Sarah's business or whatever else you decide should be a priority. But it's time to stop talking and thinking about the car loan and get it out of your life."

To their credit, they did it. They shared their screen, and I watched as they submitted the payoff amount to the lender, paying off their car loan.

I wasn't surprised they felt some relief after paying off the auto loan. It had been on their minds for a while, they agreed that it was time to pay off the loan, and they did something about it.

What *did* surprise me, though, was what happened afterward.

They showed up to their next meeting about a month later and had taken care of several important priorities:

- They realized they had enough free cash on hand to make the proposed investment in Sarah's business (an important priority of hers) *and* pay to have their estate planning documents completed (an important priority of Sam's).

- They agreed that once these items were completed, they would next direct money toward buying life insurance and increasing their retirement account contributions.

They didn't solve every single one of their financial disagreements in the weeks after they paid off their auto loan, but they made a *ton* of progress and suddenly found themselves moving forward quickly. The best part? Not only was their financial situation improving by taking care of the items on their list, but they were also feeling less out-of-sync with each other as a result.

GETTING YOUR "QUICK WIN"

Is it too much of a simplification to suggest that the act of paying off their car loan solved all of Sarah and Sam's financial problems?

Probably. But it played a much, much bigger role in moving them forward than you might expect from just seeing a $3,000 loan paid off.

It wasn't *just* that they paid off their last remaining piece of (non-mortgage) debt, although that was certainly a big deal.

It wasn't even that they finally did something financially that they both agreed on, although that was an even *bigger* deal.

It was that after years of financial stagnation, they finally got a "Quick Win" under their belt. And it gave them something to build off of.

Agreeing to pay off the car loan—and then following through to make it actually happen—gave them a "win" in their Marriage-Centered Financial Plan. It gave them a bit of momentum, which led to them tackling the next challenges head-on.

In terms of the five principles that we covered in the last chapter, taking this one step boosted them in several of the principles:

- Their financial *confidence* was boosted by giving themselves some momentum. They started to see some progress, which gave them confidence in their overall financial trajectory.

- Their financial *coordination* significantly improved because they agreed to take a specific action together for the first time in a long time.

- Their financial *commitment* went up because they didn't just talk about taking steps to improve their financial foundation as a family—they actually *did* something about it.

This one "win" helped Sarah and Sam get the ball rolling and improved their standing in three of the Five Principles of Marriage-Centered Financial Planning. This one action led them to take several other steps in the coming months, building on each of the five principles as they went and strengthening their marriage in the process.

With that in mind, let me ask you: when was the last time *you* had a financial "win?"

It doesn't necessarily need to be something big. But when was the last time you and your partner had something unambiguously good happen to your family financially—solely because of actions that you took together to make the win happen?

I'm sure a few of you can quickly think of something, which is great!

But for most of you, it's probably been a little while since you had a "Quick Win," financially speaking.

Just like with Sam and Sarah, the first step in a good Marriage-Centered Financial Plan isn't working through your biggest challenges and dealing with the biggest financial roadblocks in your way. That comes later.

Instead, the first step is getting a Quick Win under your belt to give you and your partner something to build off of. Something to immediately improve your financial confidence—the most important of the five principles. This Quick Win might feel like a small step, but it's critically important to your journey in working through some of the bigger questions and obstacles you'll face down the road.

I don't care how well-off you are financially or how in sync you feel with your spouse when it comes to money. Getting a Quick Win under your belt is important for *everyone*.

A couple that is making financial progress together is a couple that is making progress together. (Read that sentence five times fast, I dare you!) By getting the ball rolling *quickly* in starting your Marriage-Centered Financial Plan, you'll generate some instant momentum that will build your financial confidence and help accelerate your results as you work through the rest of this book.

And when I say "quick," I mean *quick*. Ideally, this would be something you could accomplish by the end of the week. If you've got a bunch of cash piling up in your savings account that you don't know what to do with, you probably could get your Quick Win within the hour.

Your Quick Win is something that should stretch you outside your comfort zone but still be very attainable in a short amount of time with a bit of effort.

PICKING YOUR "QUICK WIN" CONFIDENCE BUILDER

It doesn't even really matter *what* your Quick Win is. What truly matters is to get one under your belt quickly. But if there aren't any opportunities that immediately stand out in your mind, here are a few ideas to get you started:

Pick a side of the Money/Marriage Scale that we discussed in Chapter 1—the "money" side or the "marriage" side. Most couples tend to be more concerned about one of these two areas than the other; they are feeling really strong financially but aren't in sync with each other when it comes to money or vice versa.

If this applies to you, pick the area where you feel the weakest. If you're in bad financial shape but in alignment with your partner, aim to get a Quick Win on the "money" side. If you're fighting about money constantly or avoiding money discussions entirely, let's start on the "marriage" side.

Remember, you aren't going to solve all of your problems right out of the gate. Instead, we're looking for the *easiest thing you could do to make substantial progress in your chosen area in the next week.* Rome wasn't built in a day, and you aren't going to get your entire Marriage-Centered Financial Plan completed in a day, either. All we are doing is laying the first brick to get you a Quick Win and give you something to build off of going forward.

Pick one of the Five Principles of Marriage-Centered Financial Planning. Or more accurately, pick coordination, communication, clarity, or commitment because the mere act of getting your Quick Win is going to build your confidence by default!

Most of the time, when I introduce couples to the concept of the five principles, one or two tend to stick out as being relatively weak areas (much like how most couples have one side of the Money/Marriage Scale that is naturally weaker for them).

"I feel like we work together really well and communicate about money effectively. We just never follow through," one couple told me. So, their Quick Win was focused on commitment—picking an easy task to complete and actually *doing* it.

"We just have no idea where our money goes each month" would suggest that there could be an easy Quick Win around your money clarity. "Money is the only thing we ever fight about" might mean that it's time to get a Quick Win around communication. And so on.

And trust me, no matter if your Quick Win is focused around coordination, communication, clarity, or commitment, the mere act of getting *any* Quick Win under your belt will be enough to give you a shot in the arm of financial confidence.

It's worth noting that while I recommend picking the "money" or "marriage" side *or* picking one of the principles of Marriage-Centered Financial Planning to focus on, the end result is that your Quick Win will probably accomplish both. The only reason I differentiate between the two is just to help you brainstorm ideas and think through the question in different ways.

If you pick a Quick Win on the "money" side, you'll probably be working on your financial coordination, clarity, or commitment. If you pick a Quick Win on the "marriage" side, you'll probably be working on your financial coordination or communication.

This is one of the major reasons why getting this Quick Win is so important—it accomplishes multiple things at once!

EXAMPLES OF GOOD QUICK WINS

At the end of the day, your Quick Win can be just about *anything*, as long as it actually gets done.

Just make sure it is realistically something you could complete in the next few days. Remember, we aren't going to solve every disagreement you have with your spouse this week, and that's okay!

If it *is* realistic, then get to it. You'll feel so much better once you have your Quick Win under your belt!

But if you're looking for some ideas, here are a few that I've seen work really well for couples over the years:

Pay off your smallest debt in full. *(The "money" side of the scale; principles of coordination, clarity, and commitment.)* Just like the example from Sam and Sarah showed, there is a *lot* of power in getting rid of one of your debts in full. I don't care how small the balance is or what the interest rate is—pick your smallest credit card, student loan, or other form of debt, and pay it off *this week*. You might be surprised at the relief you will feel once you've taken this big step!

Add an extra $1,000 to your bank account. *(The "money" side of the scale; principle of clarity and commitment.)* I'm not just talking about moving money from a checking account to a savings account; I'm talking about coming up with ten Benjamin Franklins one week from now that you don't have today.

Take a few minutes and brainstorm all the ways you could come up with an extra $1,000 this week—from selling things you no longer need to picking up an extra shift or two at work, to starting a side hustle or anything in between. Choose one, then go do it.

I don't want you to strain yourself too thin by working extra hours indefinitely or selling everything you own. But you can do anything for a week … and coming up with the extra cash will be a *great* Quick Win for you. Go make it happen.

(And if $1,000 isn't an exciting enough number for you, and you think you could realistically come up with more money than that in the next seven days, you have my permission to set the number higher! The target should be realistic but still stretch you a bit.)

Get your money out of your savings account and put it to work for you. *(The "money" side of the scale; principles of coordination, clarity,* *and commitment.)* Don't go overboard on this—you should keep your emergency fund in a savings account (see Chapter 16), as well as any cash you need for short-term savings goals in the next two or three years. But if you've got a ton of money piling up in your bank accounts that you don't know what to do with, a *great* Quick Win would involve investing the extra money so that it will work harder for you in the long run. This is a great example of a Quick Win that you could accomplish in about fifteen minutes!

Pick one low-stakes financial decision that you've been putting off, make the decision, and move on. *(The "marriage" side of the scale; principles of coordination, communication, and commitment.)* When you're not on the same page about your money (or just not sure what to do next), it's really easy to lose sight of the things you *do* agree on.

But that doesn't mean that they aren't there. If you take some time to think about the pieces of your financial picture where you *are* in alignment, you might be surprised to discover how much low-hanging fruit there is.

So, if there's an aspect of your finances where you feel like you're in alignment (much like the example of Sam and Sarah's attitudes toward their car loan), focus on that area for a day or two and complete any outstanding tasks that you can related to that particular area. Doing so might not help you directly resolve any of the financial conflicts you're facing, but it will help you break out of your financial stagnation and start moving forward.

Agree with your spouse to block off one hour on your calendar to work through the money history and money scripts exercises in Part 2 of this book, and then actually follow through. *(The "marriage" side of the scale; principles of communication and commitment.)* This might be the quickest win of them all. All you need to do for now is work with your spouse to agree on a time when you both can dedicate one hour to working on the exercises I describe in the next few chapters.

The best part about the exercises in Part 2 is that they address money and marriage in a way you probably never have before. This means you'll be coming at the challenges you're facing from a different angle, one that is much less likely to lead to financial stress or money fights. It's a *great* way to start fresh and get a Quick Win under your belt … but only if you actually show up—together—and do the work.

So, your Quick Win, for now, is "just" to agree on sixty minutes with your spouse, scheduled sometime in the next seven days, where you're going to read through Chapters 4 and 5 and complete the exercises described in the chapters. That's it.

Reach out to your partner—now—and tell them you want to set aside some time to talk through your finances and set some shared money goals. I can almost feel you recoiling at the thought of doing that, and I know 90% of you won't do it. But you should.

JUST DO IT!

Now, go put this book down and actually *do* your Quick Win. You know what you need to do, and you know how to pick your Quick Win. Now it's time to make it happen!

The only reason—and I mean the *only* reason—to keep reading before you achieve your Quick Win is if you're having a hard time getting your spouse on board with the idea of working on your finances with you. If this is you, you have my permission to read the next chapter before getting your Quick Win.

By focusing on one thing at a time—even if it's a really small thing—you will begin to build your financial confidence as you start to create your Marriage-Centered Financial Plan. Your Quick Win won't be the solution to all of your money and marriage problems, but it just might be the most important step you take on the journey.

PART 2

MARRIAGE & MONEY FOUNDATIONS

Marriage-Centered Financial Planning, as the sequencing in the name suggests, doesn't start with your financial information. It starts with your marriage.

Before we work to improve your financial standing as a couple, we need to start with understanding you and your spouse's financial habits, attitudes, and values. Doing so will help you identify differences in perspectives that you have, and it will better equip you to handle these differences when you start to build your financial plan.

In Part 2, we will begin by reviewing a variety of tools, frameworks, and strategies to help you and your spouse better connect with each other. We will also identify the types of financial conflicts you are susceptible to, understand where they come from, and discuss how to handle them. We will be primarily focusing on the principles of coordination and communication.

I encourage you to read Part 2 in its entirety before beginning to implement the tools we discuss. Some couples will choose to work through each chapter from beginning to end, and others will pick the tools and frameworks that resonate with them the most. You *can* complete everything in Part 2 from beginning to end, but you don't necessarily *need* to.

On the other hand, some couples will be tempted to skip Part 2 in its entirety. This is a bad idea—even if you're not fighting about money today and are ready to get to the "good stuff" (i.e., the financial part of the book) as fast as you can, you will be leaving yourselves vulnerable to future money conflicts if you don't complete at least some of the exercises in this section.

In Chapter 4, we will discuss how to get your spouse on board with making big financial changes.

From there, we will walk through a series of tools and frameworks to help you and your spouse understand each other's money histories and money scripts (subconscious beliefs that drive you to make the financial decisions you make) in Chapter 5.

Chapter 6 builds off this material and helps you understand the nature of your financial differences.

In Chapter 7, we then walk through a framework for how to handle financial conflict when it arises in your family.

And finally, Chapter 8 discusses some more serious "red flags" to look out for and when "financial differences" shift from being something difficult but resolvable to something far more problematic.

The strategies covered in Part 2 form the foundation of a Marriage-Centered Financial Plan. Just as a strong foundation makes a building secure, the skills you and your spouse will learn will help secure your financial future as you build your net worth.

CHAPTER 4

Getting Your Spouse on Board with a Marriage-Centered Financial Plan

Every year, millions of people wake up on January 1st with a goal to lose weight during the New Year. I want you to take a moment to imagine that you are one of these people.

Let's say that you are trying to lose twenty-five pounds this year. You've thought it through, and you have a plan for how to make this happen. You're going to wake up at five a.m. every morning to exercise and cut (most of) the sugar out of your diet.

On January 2nd, you wake up and follow your plan. You get up early, hit the gym for half an hour, and follow your eating plan to the letter. You're off to a great start.

On January 3rd, your alarm goes off at five a.m. You hit snooze once, but that's okay—you get out of bed as soon as the alarm goes off the second time. As you get dressed for the gym in the dark, you hear a quiet (but very audible) sigh from your spouse as they roll over in bed, trying to get back to sleep.

On January 4th, your spouse's sigh gets a bit louder. You make sure to be extra quiet while sneaking out to the gym. When you get home from work that day, your spouse asks if you really need to set the alarm so early. You explain that you're trying to lose weight, and that's the only time of day when you know you'll get to the gym. Your spouse looks frustrated by the idea of waking up at five a.m. each day, but they tacitly agree.

On January 5th, you're still sticking to your workout plan. But when you get home, you realize it's Friday night—the night when you typically order pizza takeout for dinner. And sure enough, when you get home, a couple of pizzas are waiting for you. You decide to only have a few slices.

The next day is Saturday morning, and your spouse hits the roof when your alarm goes off at five a.m. "It's one thing for you to wake me up early during the week," they tell you. "But it's too much on the weekends."

So, you sleep in on Sunday. And just like that, your perfectly crafted plan to lose twenty-five pounds this year is in jeopardy.

Here's the thing: there are plenty of things each spouse did wrong in this anecdote. But drawing a parallel between a plan to lose weight and a plan to get in financial "shape" illustrates the importance of having your spouse support your efforts to implement a financial plan.

If you're trying to lose weight, you *don't* need your spouse to follow your game plan with you in order to succeed. They *can* if they want to, but it's not necessary.

You don't necessarily need your spouse to agree to exercise with you and eat the same foods that you eat in order for you to achieve success. In fact, forcing them to follow your plan to a T might backfire and build resentment.

But you *do* need them to understand and be supportive of your plan to achieve your goal. If your spouse complains about you setting the alarm for five a.m. each day, or keeps the house stocked with ice cream and cookies or suggests going to McDonald's twice a week…you might have success in losing weight at first, but it's going to be almost impossible for you to achieve your long-term goal.

Your spouse might have different health and fitness goals than you do, but in order for you to succeed, they *can't* be working against you.

The same is true when it comes to financial progress. You might have different attitudes and perspectives about how to improve your financial standing, and they may not be 100% bought into the idea of making a financial change with you, but they *can't* be working against you.

SUSTAINED FINANCIAL PROGRESS REQUIRES SPOUSAL SUPPORT

There are many different paths that you and your spouse can choose to travel together on the road toward a stronger marriage and a solid financial future.

But I believe it's almost impossible to make sustained financial progress if your spouse isn't supportive of your plan … and it's *much* easier to make progress if you both are working on a plan together.

The plan itself can take many different forms. Suppose you're looking to get out of credit card debt, for example. In that case, you and your spouse can choose to treat all your credit card debts as joint debts that you work to pay down together, or you can choose to treat all your personal debts as separate debts that are only the individual's responsibility to manage. Either way can work, depending on your preferences as a couple. (We will dive deeper into this debt question in Chapter 13.)

You and your spouse might not necessarily agree on what the plan should be right away, and that's completely normal. We're going to talk about a myriad of ways to solve this problem as you work through this book.

What *won't* work, though, is if you and your spouse don't agree on if there should be a plan at *all*. If you decide you want to pay off your debt as quickly as possible, and your spouse doesn't support you in this plan, it's going to be almost impossible to make the sort of financial progress you're hoping to make.

If you're looking to make a major financial change, your spouse should be on board with you. Your philosophies and specific goals might be different, but you need to be working together in some capacity.

In the context of creating a Marriage-Centered Financial Plan, this means it's okay for you and your spouse to have different priorities and expectations about what the plan will accomplish. But you should both be in agreement on getting a plan in place and working the plan together.

THE STRATEGY

So, this begs the question: if you're looking to make a big financial change in your life (like implementing a Marriage-Centered Financial Plan to put your marriage at the center of your financial decisions), how do you get your spouse on board with going through this process?

In some ways, this is a difficult question to answer, because so much of the optimal approach depends on *why* they aren't on board with making this change in the first place.

The good news is that no matter the specifics of the dynamics between you and your spouse, the strategy is the same each and every time. So, I'm going to walk you through the overall strategy first, and then discuss several tactics you might consider depending on how you see your marriage fitting into this strategy.

As you seek to get your spouse on board with making financial changes in your life, you should:

1. Do a "Four Horsemen" check
2. Understand why they aren't on board
3. Tailor your approach, and
4. Ask for a micro-commitment

Do a "Four Horsemen" Check

Don't read the apocalyptic-sounding name and shrug this off as hyperbole. For many of you, this may very well be the most important section in the entire book. You may want to bookmark this section to refer to as you complete the rest of the exercises in this book.

The "Four Horsemen of the Apocalypse," in our context, doesn't refer to the biblical end times. Rather, it's a framework developed by relationship expert Dr. John Gottman.

In his research, Dr. Gottman found that he could predict whether

GETTING YOUR SPOUSE ON BOARD

a marriage would end in divorce or not 90% percent of the time by observing the presence of one of these four communication styles, which he dubbed "The Four Horsemen."

These are *not* strictly financial in nature. Rather, each of these four communication patterns should be a warning sign *whenever* they come up in your relationship—whether it be about finances or not. But in the context of getting your spouse on board with making financial changes, I wanted to highlight each of the Four Horsemen here.

If you find yourself engaging in one of these four communication styles when talking to your spouse about making a financial change (or if your spouse responds to you using one of the Four Horsemen), that should be a *huge* sign to you that it's time to pause, re-evaluate the way you're having the discussion, and approach the discussion differently. Before continuing to try to get your spouse on board with making a financial change, you should do a quick review of each of the Four Horsemen and confirm if these are problems in the way you have discussions about money.

Below, you will find a quick overview of each of Dr. John Gottman's

Four Horsemen. As you read through the descriptions, be sure to flag any that apply to how you have these conversations with your spouse. We will revisit the Four Horsemen in the next step, "Understand Why They Aren't on Board."

Dr. Gottman's Four Horsemen

Criticism: Attacking your partner's personality or character rather than the problem you are trying to solve. It's one thing to complain about a problem; it's another to criticize the person while doing so. "Why didn't you call me when you were running late? I was worried!" is a normal complaint, but "You never think about my feelings and just do whatever you want!" crosses the line into criticism. Over time, criticism can be incredibly detrimental to your relationship.

Defensiveness: Often the response to criticism, defensiveness involves deflecting blame and avoiding responsibility for the problem. This is a very common problem in marriages that are struggling. To continue the example of the spouse who failed to call their partner to warn they were running late, an example of a defensive response to the confrontation might be "You know how busy I am. Why would you expect me to have time to call?"

Contempt: Often referred to as the most dangerous of the Four Horsemen to your relationship, contempt involves attacking your partner and placing yourself in a position of moral superiority. To treat your partner with contempt is to treat them with disrespect and meanness, either through what you say verbally or through your body language (eye rolls, etc.).

Stonewalling: Much like defensiveness is often the response to criticism, stonewalling is often the response to contempt. When you stonewall your partner, you withdraw from the conversation and stop engaging with your partner as a defense mechanism. This typically happens gradually as problems build in your relationship and things like contempt become more commonplace.

DR. JOHN GOTTMAN'S FOUR HORSEMEN

Understand Why They Aren't on Board and Tailor Your Approach

So, you've double-checked for Four Horsemen issues, and you don't think this is the reason you haven't been able to get your spouse on board with a Marriage-Centered Financial Plan. What next?

Before we start pointing fingers at your spouse, I have a hard question for you.

Is it *your* fault that your spouse isn't on board with your financial plan, or is it your *spouse's* fault?

I'm not necessarily suggesting that it *is* your fault, but I *am* suggesting that you take a few moments to think it through before pinning the blame on your spouse. Most of the time, in my experience, each spouse is at least partially to blame when something like this comes up.

More specifically, I'd like you to consider: is your spouse not on board because of the nature of the decision, or is it because of the way you're asking them to make a change?

I invite you to at least be open to the idea that your spouse might not be enthusiastic about making financial changes *both* because of the way you are asking *and* because of their attitudes about the particular financial topic in question.

Below, I've listed a variety of questions I recommend reflecting on in an attempt to understand why your spouse is resistant to the idea of financial change, as well as a suggestion on how to change your approach to increase your chances of getting them on board.

Once you have a better understanding of what's holding them back, you can better tailor your approach to help get them on board by asking them to make a "micro-commitment"—a small step in the direction of implementing a Marriage-Centered Financial Plan, which we will address at the end of the chapter. By tailoring your approach and verbalizing an "ask" that is much easier for them to say yes to, you will dramatically increase the odds that they will move forward.

Is the Problem the Way You're Asking?

Are there any signs of the "Four Horsemen" in the way you approach the subject? There's a reason that we led off this discussion with an overview of the Four Horsemen. *Nothing* will get your spouse to tune out faster than engaging in criticism or contempt when discussing their financial habits. If, after doing some honest reflection, you recognize that this has been a problem with your past approaches, you need to work on this as soon as possible.

Tailor Your Approach: Own up to how you've come up short in the way you've talked about these issues in the past, offer a sincere apology, and promise that you're committed to approaching these issues with a new tone going forward.

Are you coming on too strong? A few years ago, one of my Facebook friends started taking dietary supplements to help him get in shape from a well-known multi-level marketing company. It would be an understatement to say he quickly became obsessed with their products, mission, and culture. His social media pages soon became filled with ten to twelve weekly posts about his company's products.

A few months later, he messaged me after seeing one of my social media posts about participating in a road race the previous weekend. He told me how much he loved the company's products, how great they had been for his athletic performance, and he really pushed me to try them out for myself.

I immediately tuned him out and didn't even respond to the message.

Did my non-response have anything to do with the company and its products? Not really, to be honest. I wasn't that familiar with the company at the time and didn't have anything against them personally.

My friend just came on *way* too strong with the sales pitch. It was off-putting, and it made me tune out.

Sometimes, when you get really excited about a new way of doing things, it's easy to come on too strong in your approach. But coming on too strong, right out of the gate, can cause the exact opposite reaction that you intend.

Tailor Your Approach: Acknowledge that you've come on a little strong in the past, apologize, and indicate that while it's still really important to you to make improvements to your family's financial situation, you want to approach it in a collaborative way. Meet your spouse where they are today. And remember what got *you* excited about the opportunity in the first place—that's a *great* place to start the conversation with your spouse!

Are you not coming on strong enough? On the flip side, if you aren't clear and direct about what you're looking for, your partner might miss the message entirely. If you're looking to make a financial change, and they haven't been responsive to your desire to make this change, it's worth taking a second to make sure you are being clear and direct.

Subtlety is the enemy of good communication in a marriage. Dropping subtle clues about how you are feeling about your finances probably won't be enough to really get your partner's attention and elicit a response from them.

A very clear, direct, but friendly conversation about the change you're looking to make can go a long way to grab your spouse's attention and get them to engage in the conversation.

Tailor Your Approach: Don't be afraid to be very (but politely) direct. "Hey, I know I've mentioned in passing a few times that I wanted to work on our finances together. I don't think I've done a good job making it clear to you just how important it is to me, and I'm sorry about that. It's a big deal because [insert reason why you're so enthusiastic about making this change]."

Are you asking at the right time? If you ask or tell me anything after nine-thirty p.m., the odds of me actually retaining the conversation the next day are very low. I usually have a lot of evening client meetings, so by the time nine-thirty comes around, I'm mentally fried for the day.

If you try to have a serious conversation with me at that time, it's likely to go nowhere. Something I'd normally be amenable to during the day might be a complete nonstarter if you ask me in the evening.

The same is likely true with your partner—and it's especially true about money. Nobody likes talking about money to begin with, never mind when they're in the middle of something else or getting ready for bed!

Find an appropriate time to ask your spouse to sit down and go through your family's financial plan. Don't spring the conversation on them out of the blue; instead, ask them to put some time on their calendar in the next week to start the discussion at a time they agree to. There are several reasons why this is my favorite "micro-commitment" to ask for as a strategy to get your spouse on board, as you'll see at the end of the chapter. Minimizing the risk that you're asking at the wrong time is one of the most important reasons!

Tailor Your Approach: Ask at a different time—this one's easy! And asking about setting up a *future* time, so you're not catching them off guard, can work really well for a (relatively) intense topic like money.

Do they know how important this is to you? There's a difference between asking your spouse to do a task around the house because it needs to be done and asking them to do something because it's something that you're worried about or something that means a lot to you.

Asking your spouse to take out the trash *should* elicit a very different type of response than asking them to have a meaningful conversation with you about something you're worried about. Your spouse *should* and probably *would* sit down and have the latter conversation with you if they know what a big deal it is to you. (They should also take out the trash when you ask, but completing that item is probably less of a big deal in their mind!)

But the key is that your spouse *needs to know what a big deal it is to you* if they're going to respond appropriately. If you've been beating around the bush, dropping subtle hints, or being passive-aggressive about what you're looking to change when it comes to your family's finances, now's the time to switch up your approach and communicate a clear ask.

If you make it abundantly clear that you want their help and input to come up with a plan for how to improve your family's financial standing, and they *still* aren't willing to sit down to have the conversation with you, it's probably time to get a marriage counselor involved to help you identify what's standing in the way of you and your spouse communicating effectively with one another. But more likely than not, they'll agree to the micro-commitment if they know what a big deal it is to you.

Tailor Your Approach: Take the same recommended approach for not coming on strong enough. It's a very similar problem with a very similar solution.

Are you making demands or inviting a dialogue? Remember, your spouse gets an equal vote on how to move forward financially as a family. They probably haven't heard of Bill Nelson or Pacesetter Planning or Marriage-Centered Financial Plans before, and they aren't going to move forward with any of the stuff in this book if you demand it from them.

"Financial planning" isn't exactly a popular subject, and the approach to financial planning you'll find in this book looks very different from the stereotypes that might pop up in your head when you think about a financial planner. You need to warm them up and have a conversation before asking them to buy into a particular approach or philosophy.

I've found that the couples who have the most success getting their plan off the ground start by having a dialogue about what their spouse would be looking for in implementing this type of plan. During the course of that conversation, you can certainly talk them through the material you've found in this book and ask them to give it a shot.

But you should recognize that the initial ask needs to be less prescriptive and more focused on opening a dialogue with your partner.

Remember, you're not asking them to buy into a specific way of doing things at this point. You're asking them to buy into the idea that your marriage, and your financial state, can be stronger and that this is something worth working toward.

Tailor Your Approach: Just like with the Four Horsemen, the best bet here is to apologize for the way you've handled things previously. You should also reiterate that making financial changes for your family is a big deal to you but that you want to decide on what needs to be done together.

Is It Related to the Nature of the Financial Decision in Question?

Often, I find that making tweaks to the way you approach your partner about getting on board with a financial plan for your family will get the ball rolling. But, if you reviewed all of the above questions and didn't identify anything in your approach to change, your spouse's concerns may be related to how they feel about the underlying financial issues. Here are a few things to consider:

How do they feel about the financial issue in question? Are they not interested because they truly think that your family is in fine financial shape, so it's not worth putting in the effort to make improvements? Or are they hoping to avoid financial conversations because they're anxious or afraid about their financial state?

What looks at the surface like indifference can sometimes be hopelessness, anxiety, or other negative feelings they are suppressing in order to protect themselves emotionally. If you and your spouse are in bad financial shape, it can feel easier to ignore the problems altogether rather than confronting them head-on.

Tailor Your Approach: Acknowledge that *you're* really nervous about the state of your finances, too. If you start the conversation by being vulnerable and giving them a safe space to respond in kind, they likely will. Emphasize that it's okay that neither of you have all the answers right now and that it will take some time to right the ship—but that you want to start sooner rather than later.

Is the nature of the decision something they feel personally responsible for? Relatedly, they might not be engaging in conversations about personal finance if they feel like they've messed up financially in the past. If they feel at fault (or if they think that *you* think they're at fault), they're much more likely to disengage from the conversation.

It's much easier, after all, to avoid our shortcomings than it is to confront them head-on. That's not a reason to avoid talking about your family's financial situation going forward, of course, but it could explain why they aren't engaging in the conversation.

And whenever these sorts of issues are at play, it changes the way you need to have the conversation. You need to be especially careful not to point fingers or play the blame game to get them on board.

One of the great things about the Marriage-Centered Financial Planning process is that we don't start the conversation by focusing on the specific financial problems and stresses you are facing. You're going to start with you, your spouse, your relationship, and connecting at a deeper level.

Tailor Your Approach: Emphasize that you're not interested in criticizing any financial choices either of you have made in the past. Instead, you're looking to create a future vision for your family and make the financial moves you need to make today to get there. You can't change what's happened in the past, but you *can* chart a new path forward from there.

Do they have specific concerns with the solution you are proposing? If they have a strong affiliation for a different financial school of thought than the one you have, it may be that they are so committed to the way they do things that they aren't willing to talk about making a change.

For example, there's a group of investors that are rabid fans of index investing first espoused by the Vanguard mutual fund company and its founder, Jack Bogle. They call themselves the "Bogleheads," and they are irrationally passionate about the way they invest. (You might think this is hyperbole, but a few quick Google searches will show you it is *not*.)

If you try to talk a Boglehead into investing in an individual company stock or an actively managed mutual fund, they won't even entertain the conversation. They couldn't be less interested in either of those options, so they will react like it's not even worth their time to consider them.

So, if your spouse has strong perspectives about how to handle personal finance and feels like you are trying to talk them into something else, they may be preemptively shutting down the conversation because they're just not interested in a different solution.

(By the way, much love to my Boglehead readers. The investment philosophy I use with my clients is heavily influenced by the Boglehead philosophy. I tease you because I care!)

Tailor Your Approach: Focus on your desired outcome, not the specific solution. Remember, your money isn't the goal or the destination in a Marriage-Centered Financial Plan—it's the sail in the sailboat that helps you get there. Focus the conversation on what you want your future to look like and get buy-in to that vision first. Then, you'll have more luck discussing the solution you use to get there.

Do they see the payoff on the other side? Most people welcome a conversation about money with the same sense of enthusiasm they'd have for a trip to the dentist to fix a root canal. So sometimes, when a spouse approaches them asking to sit down to talk through their family's financial plan, their immediate reaction is something along the lines of "that sounds miserable. I don't want to do that! Maybe we can put it off."

If you view financial planning as a chore, it's not going to get done—and if it *does* somehow get done now, you almost definitely won't stick with the plan over time. It's really important to focus on the *why* behind the changes you're looking to make so that your spouse can clearly see the payoff on the other side.

Tailor Your Approach: If you're concerned that your spouse is too focused on the current reality of your financial situation to see the payoffs down the road, I recommend you start with the mission statement exercises I lay out in Chapter 9. You might be surprised how quickly your spouse tunes in once you start dreaming about your future together!

What are *their* financial priorities? So far, we have centered most of this conversation around the financial priorities you have for your family and how to get your spouse on board.

But how well can you articulate how your spouse feels or thinks about your family's financial situation? Do you understand how your spouse feels about the current lay of your financial land? Are you addressing your spouse's perspective in your approach?

Your spouse isn't coming into this conversation with a blank slate; rather, they are bringing their money history and money scripts to the table, and some of their perspectives relating to these things may be holding them back. (You'll learn all about how to handle money histories and money scripts in the next few chapters.)

The approach I teach in this book will help you and your spouse find common ground in the way you approach your family's finances. But if you're having a hard time getting your spouse to sit down and have the initial conversations with you, you should think through their perspectives in advance and tailor your approach accordingly.

Tailor Your Approach: If you're not sure what their financial priorities are, ask them! Get the conversation started with what *they're* looking for and use this as a launch pad for getting a Marriage-Centered Financial Plan in place.

Ask for a Micro-Commitment

Once you've done your homework to make a best guess about where the conversation has fallen short before, and you've decided how you're going to tailor your approach, the final step is to start the conversation again.

But before you do, it's important to keep in mind exactly what it is you're asking your spouse to do in this conversation.

At the end of the day, you want to get them on board with the idea of a Marriage-Centered Financial Plan. But if all of the "tailor your approach" suggestions above didn't make it clear, that *isn't* what I would lead with.

Instead, you want to start the conversation by asking for something small. Something that's *very* easy and appealing for them to say yes to. In other words, you want to ask them to make a micro-commitment.

When I say "micro-commitment," I mean a commitment that is small, easy to make, and something they should easily say yes to. You're not asking them to do a bunch of work to put together a financial plan right out of the gate—that's too big of an ask for someone who isn't on board yet.

Instead, you want to ask them to take the first step with you. And as I alluded to above, the recommended first step is to ask them to set up some time with you, in the next week, to talk about how your family could handle money better.

Don't worry about the specifics of what you're going to talk about in the follow-up conversation; the next several chapters will walk you through the things that could be included, and you can pick and choose the material you think will resonate with your spouse the most. Just ask to get some time on the books in the next week so that the conversation can happen.

In making this specific ask—and especially if you make the ask while tailoring your approach—you should be removing all their doubts and fears from the equation. You're not asking them for anything big; all you're asking them to do is set up some time to talk with you. That's it.

That *should* be a very easy thing for them to say yes to (although, depending on your schedules, it might be a little difficult to actually find a time that works for you). By tailoring your approach and focusing on a micro-commitment, you're taking the first steps to getting them on board to work with you financially.

CHAPTER 5

Understanding Your Money History and Money Scripts

Money is a very emotionally charged topic. In order to better understand how you and your spouse can overcome your financial differences and implement a Marriage-Centered Financial Plan, you need to start by examining yourself.

Case in point: the story of Tanya and Tom, a couple who constantly fought about, of all things, how much cash they kept in their checking account.

Tom and Tanya got married about two years before I first met them. Like many couples, they decided to combine all of their financial accounts after they tied the knot, and, for a while, it seemed like they were doing very well.

Sometimes, when you move in with your partner for the first time, things seem like they're perfect. It feels so nice to be together all the time, and you start to wonder how you ever used to live apart from each other.

But then, one day, you notice how your spouse always kicks their shoes off right in front of the front door and never bothers to put them away. (This may or may not be, but definitely is, something that I'm guilty of...)

And just like that, the illusion of a perfect marriage is over. You might not have noticed your spouse's shoe storage habits before, but now, it drives you crazy until you snap at them one day.

In the financial world, Tanya and Tom's "shoes in front of the door" issue was the amount of cash Tom wanted to keep in their bank account.

It wasn't that he spent everything they earned (although he was definitely the "spender" in their marriage; we'll talk more about that in the next chapter). He just hated keeping cash in the bank account where it wouldn't earn much interest.

So, each and every month, as soon as their credit cards were paid off, he'd draw their checking account down to almost zero and move as much money as he could into their family's investment accounts.

Tom was looking to invest as much as he possibly could. He wanted their family to keep a bare-bones emergency fund, almost no cash in their checking account, and put everything else into the stock market. To Tom, cash kept on hand was money wasted. He was always looking for the bigger, better deal when it came to how their money worked for them.

And this made Tanya very nervous.

Tanya highly valued financial stability. It wasn't that she needed to have $50,000 in her checking account at all times. But she wanted to keep a healthy enough buffer so they would never be in danger of overdrafting and would always have enough cash that they could immediately spend in case of emergency. She also placed a lot of value in having a fully funded emergency fund with enough cash to cover six months of expenses.

Their money management approaches were directly at odds with each other. And because Tom was the more hands-on spouse, he tended to take charge and move the vast majority of money out of their checking account without discussing it with Tanya first. Which, needless to say, led to a *lot* of financial fights in their household.

When Tom and Tanya first came to me looking for help handling their financial differences, I asked them a very simple, straightforward question that neither of them had ever taken the time to think about before.

"Tom," I said. "*Why* is it so important for you to keep as little cash on hand as possible and invest as much as possible?"

His answer surprised me, and it surprised Tanya even more.

After taking a few seconds to think about it, Tom told us about his experiences growing up in Eastern Europe after the fall of the Soviet Union. Some of the first money memories he had were that of dramatic inflation. He remembered his parents talking about the prices of goods their family needed to survive, doubling or tripling in very short amounts of time, and how his family was never sure how they would be able to get by.

When Tom was growing up in his home country, inflation was so bad that cash was essentially worthless. Keeping money in cash wasn't all that much better than throwing money down the garbage disposal.

Tom had internalized the fear of cash becoming worthless, which drove two seemingly contradictory financial behaviors.

First, he wasn't hesitant to spend his hard-earned money today. It wasn't that he wanted to waste money, but because he had grown up in a world where the prices for goods weren't stable in the short term, he wasn't afraid to spend money today when he saw a good deal … even if it wasn't in the budget. Spending money today, rather than waiting until tomorrow, was like making hay while the sun shined.

And second, any money that *was* saved *needed* to be invested, according to Tom, so that it had the best possible chance of being worth more in the future. Based on his experiences with money as a child, Tom wanted to avoid cash to protect his family's future financial security.

Now, the financial risks in the United States today look very different from the economies of Eastern Europe in the early 1990s. I'm not saying that Tom was *right* in making the financial decisions he made for his family based on having these perspectives. But by having this conversation, Tanya gained a much deeper understanding and appreciation for why her husband managed money the way he did. It turned the conversation about keeping money in their checking account from a fight to one that led them to form a deeper connection in their marriage.

By understanding Tom's money history and how it affected his financial management tendencies today, we were able to identify the right approach to manage the risks he perceived in keeping cash on hand with Tanya's desired flexibility, while working on the underlying money scripts that caused Tom to have anxiety about keeping cash on hand. Neither one of them got exactly what they wanted. Their emergency fund was bigger than Tom would have ideally wanted, but not as big as Tanya would have chosen for herself—but we were able to tailor an approach to respect Tom's money history in a way that didn't hold their family back financially.

By better understanding your own personal money values and attitudes and how you developed these perspectives, you'll be able to better connect with your spouse and have an easier time identifying the root causes of your financial differences.

That doesn't necessarily mean you should be doing the work described in this chapter on your own. On the contrary, I've noticed over the years that very few conversations can move the needle in a Marriage-Centered Financial Plan faster than a conversation about you and your spouse's money histories.

I encourage you to discuss the items in the rest of this chapter with your spouse. A few ground rules before we begin:

- The goal in understanding your money attitudes and how you developed them over time is to learn more about yourself and your partner. When it is your partner's turn to explore their money histories, your job is to a) ask the questions I describe in this chapter, and b) listen to their responses. No more, no less. Create the space for them to explore these concepts, listen to their answers, and learn more about the person you've committed to spending the rest of your life with. And, as always, be especially careful not to let the Four Horsemen creep into the conversation.

- This is not a problem-solving discussion. Often when exploring your money histories, some challenging topics will come up. That's completely normal—your job is to listen and understand your spouse's perspective. Remember, your spouse is not a problem that needs to be solved. They're a person who, in all likelihood, has had a *lot* of life experiences that cause them to manage money in a particular way. There are no problems to solve in the discussion, just facts to learn. In the next few chapters, we'll talk about how to use what you learn in exploring your money histories to help you resolve financial arguments together. But for now, you're just listening.

- There is absolutely no reason and no excuse to fight when having this conversation. If money is something you and your spouse frequently fight about, you need to put down the metaphorical sword for a moment. Exploring your money histories is a way to better understand yourself and your spouse and the reasons why you each have different perspectives on the financial issues at hand; it's not something that will solve the financial disagreements you're currently facing today. (Again, we'll get there in the next few chapters.)

- Exploring your money history requires you to be open and vulnerable, not just with your partner but with yourself. As such, this conversation needs to be a judgment-free zone. We often carry around decades worth of shame and blame for things that have happened in our past. For this conversation, I'm asking you to set these things aside. (Easier said than done, I know.) Don't judge your partner for experiences they will share with you about their money histories, and you shouldn't judge yourself, either.

HOW DID YOU LEARN ABOUT MONEY GROWING UP?

Most of us were never formally taught how to handle money as part of a school curriculum. This means the way most of us learned about money was from our experiences growing up.

If money was really tight in your family as a child, this inevitably will influence the way you view certain financial decisions today. If money was something your parents constantly fought about, you are carrying the lessons you learned from the years you spent watching this dynamic in the way you interact with your spouse about money.

I once met a woman named Britt whose top financial priority was getting a *lot* of life insurance coverage in place—not just for her but for her husband Blaine as well. Not a week went by when she wasn't subtly (or not-so-subtly) reminding her husband to send in the paperwork and schedule the underwriting exam.

Finally, her husband snapped. "I just don't understand why this is such a big deal for you. We don't have kids; we don't have a mortgage. Why do we need life insurance so badly?"

It took a little while—and a whole lot of bickering—to get to the ultimate answer: Britt's mother had been diagnosed with an aggressive form of cancer back when Britt was in high school. Her mom passed away about six months later.

One of the only vivid memories she had of her mom getting her diagnosis was her mom's immediate reaction. She remembers her mom turning to her dad, tearing up, and apologizing for not getting more life insurance coverage.

Needless to say, Blaine left the conversation with a much better understanding of why Britt was so focused on getting their own life insurance coverage in place. He took the next steps to set up his policy the following day.

By taking the time to have a conversation about your money history, you'll learn a lot about why you view money the way you do. Consider discussing the following questions with your partner to explore your money histories:

- What's the first memory you have involving money?

- Growing up, money was ______________.

- What did you learn about money from your parents/guardians? How open were they with you (and each other) about money?

- Who taught you about money when you were growing up?

Remember, all you're doing for now is talking about your past. There will be plenty of time to extrapolate the items you uncover to understand how they are shaping your present-day financial issues and arguments. But for now, all you're looking to do is understand where your partner is coming from and how they arrived at their current attitudes about money.

MONEY SCRIPTS

For some couples, answering a few open-ended questions like the ones above will take you a long way to developing an understanding of why you each manage money the way you do. But if you're looking for a more rigorous analysis of how your money history affects the way you view money today, you should consider analyzing your *money scripts.*

Money scripts were developed and academically tested by a team of researchers led by financial psychologist Dr. Brad Klontz. The original academic work on money scripts was based on individuals, not couples, but understanding how your money scripts overlap (or oppose) your spouse's money scripts can help explain many of your differences in financial perspectives.

What are money scripts? In a nutshell, they are:

Unconscious beliefs about the role of money in your lives. Since we don't actively think about them, they tend to be assumptions that guide our actions unless we intentionally take the time to examine them.

Developed in childhood and often mirror the same attitudes as your parents.

Incomplete or partial truths. In each money script, there are certain components that are true but also some things that are false. For example, one common money script is that "money would solve all of my problems." There are certain grains of truth to this—if you're struggling financially, there's no denying that having more money would make a lot of things in life easier. But there are also some limits to this—having more money won't solve health problems, loneliness, or disputes in your family. (In fact, having more money might make some of these problems worse!)

Perspectives that enable you to make decisions about your finances the way you do, which means that money scripts are often responsible for the financial outcomes you have.

Capable of being changed. By understanding the money scripts that motivate you, and through understanding the degree to which they may not be objectively true, you can form a more balanced perspective on money over time.

WHAT ARE MONEY SCRIPTS?

Some examples of money scripts include statements like the following:

- People get rich by taking advantage of others.
- More money will make you happier.

- I will not buy something unless it is new.
- Money should be saved, not spent.

You may strongly agree with one or more of these statements, or you may completely disagree. The money scripts that drive your financial behavior will be different from other people's money scripts, and this certainly includes your spouse.

In the course of his research, Dr. Klontz categorized a variety of different money scripts to help readers and researchers better understand the way that we view and manage money. He identified four primary categories of money scripts:

Money Avoidance: A belief that money is bad or that you don't deserve money. Often, people with strong Money Avoidance scripts will try to avoid thinking about money and will self-sabotage their financial success.

Money Status: A belief that money equals self-worth. This often causes individuals with strong Money Status scripts to overspend on things that will display their wealth. And, for the purposes of Marriage-Centered Financial Planning, it's important to note that Money Status is often correlated with hiding spending from one's spouse.

Money Worship: This is exactly what it sounds like. People who score highly on the Money Worship money scripts view money as the solution to all of their problems. This doesn't necessarily mean that these individuals are in good financial shape, though; they often seek as much money as possible and spend most of it in pursuit of happiness.

Money Vigilance: This is the most "positive" of the money scripts, although it often comes with excessive financial anxiety or guilt. People who score highly on the Money Vigilance money scripts are diligent and mindful of their financial health, and they are highly motivated to save.

THE FOUR CATEGORIES OF MONEY SCRIPTS

Money Avoidance

- Money = bad
- I don't deserve money
- Avoid thinking about money
- Self-sabotage financial success

Money Status

- Money = self-worth
- Overspend on things that display wealth
- Sometimes correlated with hiding spending from spouse

Money Worship

- Money = the solution to all problems
- Often seek as much money as possible and spend most of it in pursuit of happiness

Money Vigilance

- Money = important to save
- Diligent of financial health
- Often comes with excessive financial anxiety or guilt

I recommend that you and your spouse go through and identify which money script categories you most align with; you can access a tool to help you do this at marriagecenteredmoney.com/resources. By understanding your partner's primary money scripts, you can better understand what motivates them financially.

As you might imagine, if you score highly on "Money Worship" and your spouse scores highly on "Money Avoidance," this is going to create some discord in the way you manage money as a family—unless you intentionally tailor your family's money management to account for each of your money scripts. So, the first step is to determine which are the primary motivating money scripts for you and your spouse.

And remember, money scripts are not universal truths, which means they are capable of being changed. If you realize you score strongly on the Money Worship money scripts, you might identify this as a problem and recognize the ways it is holding your family back financially. You can then start to work on your money scripts to find a more balanced way to manage your finances over time.

Once you know you and your spouse's money scripts, you should take a bit of time to discuss the results with your spouse.

What did you learn about the way you view money as a result of going through this exercise? How do you think your money scripts manifest in the financial conflicts you have as a family? What can you do differently as a family to manage money going forward now that you have an increased awareness and understanding of your money scripts?

By reviewing the differences you and your spouse have when it comes to your money scripts, you will begin to understand the reasons that you often aren't on the same financial page. For now, just focus on trying to understand these differences and working on your personal money scripts as needed.

Much like with your money histories, don't worry too much about the differences between you and your spouse when it comes to your money scripts at first. Instead, you should seek to understand how your money scripts manifest in your personal financial decision-making, identify any steps you'd like to take in working through your more problematic money scripts (and encourage your partner to do the same on their own), and go through the rest of this book to bring you and your spouse together while you work on your money scripts on your own. Again, you can access a tool to help you identify your primary money scripts at marriagecenteredmoney.com/resources.

START IN THE REARVIEW
MIRROR, THEN LOOK AHEAD

Your money histories and money scripts are important tools that can help you and your spouse get on the same financial page. You *should* spend some time trying to understand why you think about money the way you do today.

But I also don't want you to get too bogged down in what's happened in the past. Marriage counseling and financial therapy can be incredibly effective if done properly and in the right circumstances. But the problem I sometimes see with couples working with marriage counselors or therapists is that it becomes very easy to get stuck in the past.

It's really important to understand how your history—and the scripts that developed from this history—affect the way you view the world today. But the goal isn't to go back and fix mistakes that have happened before; instead, you want to take what you've learned about your past and use it to help you move forward.

In that sense, discussing your money history and identifying your money scripts are a little bit like looking in the rearview mirror while you're driving a car. It's an incredibly useful tool to have in the right circumstances, and everybody needs to spend *some* time looking in the rearview mirror while they're driving.

But don't get stuck constantly looking backward. Glance back, learn what you need to learn, and then use this information to help you move forward in handling the financial disagreements you're facing today.

CHAPTER 6

Understanding Your Financial Differences

One day, Jennifer woke up with a headache. Not just an ordinary headache, but a headache that was so severe that she was afraid she was seriously ill.

So, she did what most of us would do: she opened her phone, pulled up Google, and searched for "headache causes."

This led her, of course, to the absolute last website in the world that Jennifer should have landed on if she was worried about a vague medical problem: WebMD.

If you've ever been on WebMD for your own medical inquiries, you know what happened next.

As Jennifer read through the potential causes, her eyes grew wide. "According to WebMD, my headache could be caused by anything from 'dehydration' to 'a brain tumor,'" she said to herself.

Did Jennifer know that she probably didn't have a brain tumor? Yes. But it freaked her out just enough to do what she probably should have done from the beginning—she called her doctor and scheduled an appointment.

Later that day, Jennifer was waiting in the examination room when her doctor came in to greet her.

"So, what brings you in today?" he asked as he scrubbed his hands and sat down on the chair next to her.

"I woke up with a bad headache," she replied.

"I'm sorry to hear that," the doctor answered. "Here's a prescription for Azithromycin."

———

I'll come clean—the story about Jennifer is completely made up. But in the context of money and marriage, it serves a very important purpose.

Did you notice anything in the way that I told Jennifer's story that might immediately suggest it's not real?

Jennifer told the doctor she had a headache, and the doctor didn't respond by asking additional questions. No looking for other symptoms, no sticking the light up her nose to see what's going on up there … nothing. He just handed her a prescription.

It's a ridiculous example to think about in a medical context. We all know this isn't the way doctors work.

But here's the key: this is *exactly* how most of us work when it comes to money and marriage topics.

You wake up one day and realize that something about the way you and your spouse are managing money together isn't working well. You don't know if it's a big deal or not, so you do a quick Google search, end up on the financial planning equivalent of WebMD (of which, unfortunately, there are quite a few), and maybe even call a financial professional.

But unlike doctors, most financial professionals are *very* quick to pull out the prescription pad and start doling out quick fixes.

If you were Jennifer, would you have taken the prescription the doctor wrote for you? Odds are, you wouldn't.

Why is that?

Because you weren't thoroughly diagnosed first.

I learned this metaphor and framework of "diagnosing before prescribing" from Carl Richards, two-time bestselling financial author,

New York Times personal finance columnist, and founder of *The Society of [Financial] Advice*. Whenever I'm working to advise a couple on making a difficult financial decision, I always remind myself to get enough information to make the right diagnosis before I start writing financial prescriptions.

And while Richards's metaphor is applicable to so many areas of financial planning, I think it's especially pertinent to handling financial differences with your spouse.

DIAGNOSE FIRST, PRESCRIBE SECOND

It's *completely* normal for you to have different financial habits, attitudes, and values than your spouse—in fact, some research suggests that people are *likely* to choose spouses who are "opposite" from them financially. But it's critical for the future of your marriage that you learn to handle these differences the right way.

Whenever we feel out of sync with our partner, our natural inclination is to go into "fix-it" mode. We identify there's a disconnect, and we want to fix it. This is true of any difference or argument you have with your spouse, and it is certainly true of financial differences.

Before you start taking action to get on the same financial page, we need to first understand the nature of your financial differences. By diagnosing what the difference is really about, you'll have a much easier time implementing the right solution.

This brings me back to the example of Jennifer and her doctor.

If the doctor were going to give Jennifer a thorough diagnosis, he would have done two things differently:

- First, he would have explored her medical history. He would have asked her questions about headaches she's had in the past, any family history of common causes of the type of headaches she was having, and so on.

- Then, he would have examined her for other symptoms to understand the scope and nature of the problem she was having.

Then, and only then, would he decide on a prescription or another course of action.

In the context of money and marriage disputes, you should follow the exact same process:

- First, you should examine and understand your money histories and money scripts. We completed this in the previous chapter.

- Then, you should understand the dynamics of the current disagreement you and your spouse are facing in the context of your money histories and money scripts, so you can appropriately diagnose it.

Once you understand how your past may be affecting the current conflict in the form of your money histories or your money scripts, and you identify the type of conflict you're facing, you'll be much better equipped to prescribe the right solution.

We've talked about the money history piece of the puzzle. Now, let's talk about the types of financial conflicts couples experience.

Financial arguments and disagreements tend to fall into certain patterns. By learning to identify the patterns and how they match the money fights that you and your spouse face, you will be able to gain a deeper understanding of the root of the problem and will be able to better identify the right solution.

THE MOST COMMON TYPES
OF FINANCIAL DIFFERENCES

I've identified the most common financial differences I see between couples and described them below. You will likely find that some of these are much more relevant to your family than others.

By reviewing these differences, identifying the ones that are particularly prevalent in your family, and eliminating others, you'll have a much easier time taking action to get on the same financial page efficiently. You'll use what you learn about your financial differences as you work through the conflict resolution framework described in the next chapter, and more broadly as you work through the rest of the exercises in this book.

1. Saver versus Spender

Whenever we talk about financial differences between spouses, this is the one that most commonly comes up in discussion.

Within a couple, there is typically one spouse who, when given the choice, would rather save money for the future than spend it today. I'm not just talking about someone who saves money because they know they should; rather, the "saver" in a couple is someone who actually *enjoys* saving money. Seeing their bank account balances grow over time actively brings them joy.

On the other side of the coin, the "spender" isn't necessarily opposed to saving money, but when given the choice between saving money for the future or spending it on something today, they'd much prefer to spend the money now.

2. Possessions versus Experiences

Let's set aside preferences about saving for a second and consider the money you and your spouse decide you want to spend for your family. Outside of the bare essentials you need to spend money on to provide for your family, how do you prefer to spend money?

If you had an extra $1,000 to spend, would you spend it on a possession for your family (a piece of furniture, a TV, or a computer), or would you spend it on a family vacation or a few trips to a ballgame?

When putting together your wedding registry, were you more excited to have people gift you some kitchenware or contribute to a honeymoon fund?

Some of us are more naturally inclined to want to spend money on things or possessions. Some of these things can be practical, while others may be more frivolous. (And that isn't necessarily a bad thing!)

On the other hand, other people have a bigger desire to spend their money on experiences for themselves, their family, or others.

This isn't one of the more common differences I see between

couples. Usually, couples tend to be fairly well aligned on their philosophy between spending on things versus experiences. But when these differences *do* exist, they tend to produce a *lot* of money fights. Being able to diagnose this difference, therefore, is critical.

3. Value versus Quality

When you decide to spend money on something, how do you approach your buying decision?

Do you like to "shop the sales," negotiate with the seller, and overall try to find the best deal that you can? Or are you less concerned with how much you spend and more concerned with the quality of what you are purchasing?

Some people are highly motivated by the bottom-line cost. When given the choice between a cheaper, more basic option versus a nicer, more expensive option, they'll choose the least expensive option every time. Why buy your clothes at Nieman Marcus or Nordstrom when you can buy a perfectly fine pair of jeans at Walmart?

For someone who emphasizes quality, the bottom-line price isn't as important as what you get for the money you spend. This preference might have to do with the expected longevity of the purchase ("Why spend $200 for a couch from IKEA when I could get a couch that will last for a decade for $500?"), or just the overall look and feel of the product.

As you might imagine, if you and your spouse fall on opposite ends of this spectrum, it can complicate decisions about spending. Once again, you'll need to find the right balance when making these decisions to ensure your family's financial plan will work for you over time.

4. Hands-On versus Hands-Off

This difference has to do with how actively you like to manage your finances on a day-to-day, week-to-week, or month-to-month basis.

Most couples tend to have one member who likes to take a more active role in managing their money and one who would rather not need to get into the weeds to handle the family's financial tasks.

As you might imagine, I'm naturally the more hands-on financial spouse in my household. As a financial planner, I actively *enjoy* handling money and paying attention to the details, so most (but not all!) of the time, I'm the one paying the bills and managing the investment accounts.

It's worth noting that there can be a few different reasons *why* one member of the family is more inclined to be hands-on with money. Some of these aren't a problem at *all*, but they're good to be aware of. Others, though, are signs of broader issues at play. Some explanations of this type of financial difference include:

- One person likes taking responsibility for these tasks. This isn't inherently a problem, and it's a normal difference to have.

- One spouse worries a lot more about the finances, which makes them more interested in having a hands-on role. As you implement your Marriage-Centered Financial Plan, my hope is that some of this anxiety starts to decrease!

- One spouse is more inclined to avoid money, so they'd rather let their spouse handle the finances. While it's perfectly okay for one spouse to be less involved, we *don't* want you to actively be avoiding money.

- One spouse is more motivated to make financial progress than the other. This one can feel like it's working in the short run for both the hands-on and hands-off spouse, but in the long run, it's likely to hold you back financially, in your relationship, or both.

Note: This difference isn't referring to making financial *decisions* but rather executing financial tasks. Major financial decisions for your family *should* be made together, with each spouse getting an equal vote.

5. Independence versus Interconnected

Does being married mean that you start making spending decisions together with your spouse? If so, does it mean you make *all* of your spending decisions together, or do you each retain some financial independence? Do you combine some or all of your bank accounts with your spouse?

Tying the knot and committing yourselves to each other doesn't necessarily mean you need to commit to making all of your spending decisions together. Some spouses desire a high degree of financial autonomy after they get married. Deciding to keep some or all of your money separate from your spouse *can* be the right choice for you to make—if you and your partner both value your financial independence from each other, and you have a clear process in place to achieve your shared goals as a family.

The challenge, though, is what happens when one spouse is much more inclined to combine money than the other and wants to forgo financial independence in the name of household unity. This type of financial difference with your spouse can lead to difficulties in making financial decisions as a family.

If you compromise too much in the direction of financial independence, it can leave the spouse who wants to be financially interconnected feeling abandoned. If you compromise too far in the direction of interconnecting your finances, it can leave the spouse who wants more autonomy feeling trapped.

6. Security versus Freedom

This one usually isn't as obvious at the surface for most couples, but I find the more I talk to couples about these concepts, the more they tend to realize that this difference applies to them.

As you'll see in Chapter 9, one of my favorite questions to ask couples is: "Why is money something that's important to you?"

And almost every single time I've ever asked a couple this question, one spouse has replied with "security," "safety," or a synonym for these words, and the other replies with "freedom," independence," or a similar concept.

Within marriages, it's common for one spouse to be financially motivated by the desire to keep the family safe and secure financially. To this spouse, things like avoiding debt, having a healthy emergency fund, and having adequate levels of insurance coverage are *really* important.

On the flip side, the spouse more motivated by financial freedom is primarily interested in seeing their money growing and working for them. To this spouse, debt, for example, is a tool to use to help you build wealth rather than something that should be avoided entirely.

A good Marriage-Centered Financial Plan will give you *both* financial security and financial freedom, and we're going to go through how to find the right balance in a *lot* of detail in Chapter 16. The key, as we will discuss, is working on building your financial security and financial freedom by following the right sequence of steps, in the right order, and appropriately prioritizing these items as a family.

7. Good versus Evil

Is having more money *actually* a good thing? Or is the pursuit of wealth something that's likely to lead your family to moral ruin?

As we know from our discussion on money scripts, most of us were taught some particularly strong positive or negative things about money from a young age that we have internalized. Some of us were taught about the virtue of saving, living frugally, and building a family nest egg. Others were taught that money is the root of all evil and that becoming rich would corrupt your spirit.

Naturally, then, it's common for spouses to have different perspectives on whether money is a force for good in their family or a force for evil. Finding the right way to balance these perspectives and address each of your needs in this context is critical not just for your family's future financial health but for the strength of your marriage as well.

A NOTE ON GENDER DIFFERENCES

Talking about gender roles and gender differences is inherently a complicated subject to discuss these days, and I intentionally haven't placed a strong focus on gender throughout this book.

But, there are a few academically validated concepts related to financial differences and gender that *do* create problems for couples sometimes, so I think it's important to briefly discuss the role of gender in money fights.

Discussing gender roles and financial attitudes is difficult because unless it's done carefully, the conversation can quickly devolve into stereotypes, which isn't helpful for anyone. I never recommend *starting* conversations with your spouse by examining your different financial habits and attitudes through the lens of gender dynamics. But if you've tried most of the tactics in this book and aren't making headway, it's worth considering whether there are underlying gender dynamics that should be addressed in this conversation.

With that in mind, here are a few specific sticking points I sometimes see couples struggling with, as well as some tips to get started working through them with your spouse:

Men and women tend to get different emotional benefits from money. Academic research has shown that men and women often have different motivating factors that drive them to improve their financial standing. Specifically, men are typically more likely to view money as a vehicle of freedom or autonomy, and women are more likely to view money as either a vehicle of security or a way to show love. Again, there are (obviously) exceptions to this, but it's worth keeping these perspectives in mind when you analyze financial differences in your own family.

When She Makes More. Personal finance expert Farnoosh Torabi published *When She Makes More: Ten Rules for Breadwinning Women* in 2014, and I consider it to be the seminal work on navigating financial differences related to gender roles in the 21st century. Torabi goes into a *ton* of academically validated strategies for how to handle the real-world implications that come up in families where the wife is the primary breadwinner. If you suspect these sorts of challenges may be an issue in your marriage, I can't recommend reading her book enough, and we're going to revisit some of the lessons from this book in Chapter 11.

Again, I don't recommend gender norms being the primary lens you use to review your family's financial differences—the list of the seven most common financial differences we spent most of this chapter reviewing is the best place to start. But if you're having some sort of financial disconnect and it seems like there's something deeper going on, it's worth exploring whether you could be having some disagreements related to gender roles. Right or wrong, like it or not, these types of issues sometimes come up, and it's important to address them in the correct context.

Whatever the nature of the financial disputes you are having, it's important to diagnose the specific challenges you are facing before you try to implement the right solution. By correctly identifying the problem at the outset, you're much more likely to arrive at the right solution faster.

Hopefully, understanding the common types of financial differences will help you identify the problems that arise in your household when you see them. Only once you've identified the type of difference you're experiencing (and ideally what money scripts are causing the difference) can you work to resolve the conflict—which we'll cover in the next chapter.

CHAPTER 7

Financial Conflict Resolution

Armed with the foundation you've built in the past few chapters about understanding you and your spouse's money history, money scripts, and financial differences, you're now ready to tackle financial conflict resolution.

The problem, though, is that the way most of us were taught how to resolve conflicts is often the wrong approach. Allow me to illustrate how most people go wrong when attempting to resolve conflicts with perhaps the silliest example imaginable: an orange.

Imagine you and two friends rented a house on the beach for a weekend. You walk into the kitchen on Sunday morning only to find that your two friends are fighting over who gets the last orange in the fruit basket.

Being the good friend you are, you decide to step in and help your friends resolve their dispute. And so, you draw upon everything you've ever been taught about solving arguments, and you encourage them to compromise.

In the extremely unlikely event you've managed to make it this far in life without learning what a compromise is, here's a brief refresher: in a compromise, each person gets a little bit of what they want and gives up a little bit of what they want.

So, you think to yourself; this is very straightforward.

Reaching for a knife, you take the orange from the table, cut it in half, and triumphantly hand one half to the first friend and the rest of the orange to the other friend. Problem solved ... or so you think.

As it turns out, getting half of the orange makes *both* of your friends angry. Neither one of them are content to only have half of the orange. Your attempt at getting your friends to compromise failed.

Frustrated, you turn to your friends and ask, "Why aren't you happy with your half of the orange? I know you didn't get everything you wanted, but you at least get something!"

"Well, I was planning on scraping the zest off of the entire orange to use for a recipe I wanted to make," one of your friends responds. "And the recipe calls for the zest of one whole orange. If I only use my half of the orange, I won't have enough."

Your second friend smiles upon hearing this remark. "I was going to squeeze the orange to make juice for our breakfast. Only using half the fruit wouldn't make enough juice."

Happily, your friends realize there's an easy solution. Your first friend scrapes the zest off of both halves of the orange, and your other friend then squeezes both halves to make juice. Your attempt at compromise may have been a spectacular failure, but each of your friends got what they were looking for.

APPROACHES TO CONFLICT MANAGEMENT

The example of the orange may be somewhat silly, but it illustrates an important concept: while compromise can play a role in resolving conflicts, it should *not* be the only tool you attempt to use with your partner when you have disagreements.

By understanding the *why* behind the conflict and the nature of the disagreement, you can increase your chances of finding a win-win outcome for everyone involved. This is the reason we've spent so much time trying to understand your money history, money scripts, and financial differences so far in this book. Armed with this information, you're much more likely to be able to identify and implement a solution that works well for both you and your spouse.

According to the Thomas-Kilmann Conflict Mode Instrument (TKI), there are five types of approaches you can take to resolve conflicts within your marriage, each of which vary in the degree of assertiveness and cooperativeness that you and/or your spouse will employ to resolve the issue. Some of them should be used more frequently than others, but all of them can be useful tools to use depending on the nature of the conflict in question. Once we review each of the Five Styles of Conflict Management, we will discuss *how* to resolve your conflicts as a family.

THE FIVE STYLES OF CONFLICT MANAGEMENT (TKI)

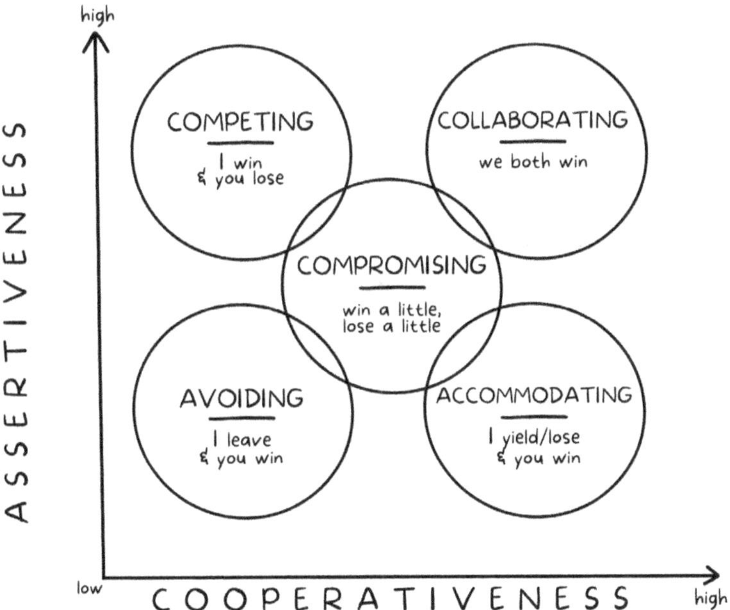

1. Competing conflict resolution style *(high levels of assertiveness, low levels of cooperativeness)*. When you use this style, you are more concerned with winning the argument by using your power in the relationship than you are with preserving the relationship itself.

Utilizing this type of conflict resolution obviously creates problems of its own and is generally only appropriate in emergency situations.

Example of appropriate use: You are angry at your spouse for overspending. When you confront them about it, you discover that the source of overspending is a drug addiction you were not aware of. Under a competing style of conflict resolution, you immediately shut off their access to your joint bank accounts (exerting control to stabilize the situation, even if it angers your spouse) while you get them the help they need.

2. Avoiding conflict resolution style (*low levels of assertiveness, low levels of cooperativeness*). When you use this style, you are avoiding dealing with the issue, and in some cases, you may even be in denial that there is a problem at all. When this occurs, both you and your spouse's needs in the conflict will not be fulfilled.

This style might feel like the easiest approach in the short term because it avoids a fight about money, but in the long term, it can create rifts in your relationship by building resentment over time.

Nevertheless, this style of conflict is acceptable for small, trivial, or petty differences where confronting your spouse about the issue will do much more damage than letting the issue go.

Example of appropriate use: You are angry at your spouse for treating a friend to a nice dinner rather than splitting the bill. This isn't something that happens regularly, and it isn't something that has a significant impact on achieving your financial goals. So, rather than picking a fight about this one-time issue, you avoid the conflict and let it go.

3. Accommodating conflict resolution style (*low levels of assertiveness, high levels of cooperativeness*). When you use this style, you typically are able to have good, meaningful discussions about the conflict at hand, but you tend to yield your point of view and "give in" to your spouse.

This can be a very useful style to use when preserving your marriage is more important than your own needs in the argument. *However*, this approach should not be used regularly. If you consistently suppress your own desires in the name of maintaining the relationship, you will grow resentful over time.

Example of appropriate use: You recognize that your spouse is burned out and overwhelmed at work. You rely on their income and have serious concerns about what your spouse changing careers and taking a pay cut would mean for your family's financial stability. But you recognize how badly their need is to make a change, so you're willing to accommodate them changing jobs and taking a slight pay cut by cutting your discretionary spending by 20% until you get settled into your new family budget.

4. Compromising conflict resolution style *(medium levels of assertiveness, medium levels of cooperativeness)*. As we've discussed, in this approach, you each get some of what you want and give up some of what you want.

On the surface, this approach seems fair, and it can work well in certain circumstances. Notably, compromises *don't* always need to be split 50/50—as long as each of you is getting a little and giving a little, it is a compromise that could work. Just recognize that compromises are a zero-sum game, as illustrated in the example below.

Example of appropriate use: You and your spouse agree that you have room in your budget for $500 of personal spending per month, and you're trying to figure out how to split the $500 between the two of you for your individual spending. You could compromise and divide it right down the middle and say that each of you gets $250 to spend monthly. Alternatively, if your spouse has higher personal expenses than you do (for example, if it costs them twice as much to get their hair cut as it does for you), you could decide to compromise and give your spouse $300 of the $500 budget and keep the remaining $200 for yourself. Or, if your spouse earns significantly more money than you, you might decide that their personal spending budget should be proportional to their salary (for example, they might spend $350 in personal spending, and you might get $150).

All of these are valid compromises, but the downside is that each compromise is a zero-sum game. A dollar that your spouse gets to spend is a dollar that *you* don't get to spend.

5. Collaborating conflict resolution style (*high levels of assertiveness, high levels of cooperativeness*). This is the ideal win-win scenario. By focusing on the underlying needs ("I need to bake a recipe/make juice") rather than the position at hand ("I need the last orange"), both people are able to get their needs met.

However, this approach is usually the most difficult to execute because it requires each party to collaborate with each other *and* clearly articulate their needs.

As you begin your journey to implement a Marriage-Centered Financial Plan, you need to be particularly careful not to default to the accommodating or avoidance conflict resolution styles because, in the short term, they often feel like the easiest way to go. While avoiding or accommodating conflict feels like the path of least resistance in the short term, these styles can lead to increasing resentment and frustration that can destabilize your relationship over time.

As an example, one of the most common places where I see couples avoiding conflict in an unhealthy way is when spouses with big saver/spender differentials keep separate bank accounts, so they have a certain amount of "no questions asked" spending money. By keeping money separate in a personal checking account, they're able to successfully avoid the conflict about how much money was spent each month.

Here's the interesting thing: when used correctly, separate bank accounts are a perfectly healthy tool to use to help manage conflict. But this *only* works in the context of a Marriage-Centered Financial Plan where you have sat down as a family, determined how much money you *need* to save as a family each month (which you'll learn how to do in Part 3), confirmed that you're able to hit these savings targets, and only *then* moved whatever is left over into your personal no-questions-asked spending accounts.

If you have separate accounts with this type of plan in place, you aren't avoiding the issue at all. You've sat down together and agreed on how much needs to be saved each month, and you've put guardrails in place to make sure this actually happens. The separate accounts in this context are just a tool that you use to help keep track of what's spendable for each spouse.

But if you're *not* doing all of those steps, you are likely using separate accounts as a way to avoid conflict over your saving and spending differences. This might work out for you in the short term, but it's likely to lead to resentment in the long term.

SETTING THE STAGE FOR FINANCIAL CONFLICT RESOLUTION

When you're ready to start working through conflicts with your spouse, it's so tempting to just sit down and dive right into the discussion at hand.

But according to Dr. Sarah Asebedo—former Financial Therapy Association president who has conducted research on financial conflict resolution for couples (and whose work inspired most of the content in this chapter)—it's important to set the stage for the conversation.

Just like you wouldn't run a 5k before taking some time to stretch first, you want to properly put yourselves in the right frame of mind so that you can more effectively and constructively work through your conflicts. This involves a few key steps:

Understand that it's normal to have money arguments. There's no such thing as permanently fixing all of your money arguments, nor is there a couple who ever stops fighting about money entirely. Understand that the feelings you are having and the struggles you are facing right now are completely and 100% normal. The work you did around reviewing your financial differences and your money scripts should show you that you aren't alone in the types of conflicts you are facing!

By accepting financial arguments as normal, you will put yourself in a state where you are better able to have productive conversations.

View money conflicts as opportunities. By taking the time to explore your money histories, money scripts, and financial differences with your spouse, you have taken the time to get to know each other at a deeper level. Even though there are some roadblocks in your way (in the form of the conflicts you are facing), you have come a long way in building better bonds, which will help you immensely as you work through the arguments at hand.

And as a side note, the reason why I asked you to work through your money histories, money scripts, and financial differences before now was so that you can refer to these conversations as you work through the conflicts you are facing. Use what you've learned about each other to try to forge new paths forward!

Balance power in the conversation. I don't care which of you is more involved in the day-to-day financial decisions, makes more money, or has more financial assets. Whenever you are sitting down to make *any* sort of financial decision, each of you has an equal say in the outcome. This can be tricky to implement effectively on your own, especially if you historically have had challenges managing power differentials in your relationship. Nonetheless, it's crucial to focus on leveling the playing field whenever you're working to resolve a conflict.

RESOLVING MONEY ARGUMENTS

Once you've each reviewed the three ways to set the stage I described above, Dr. Asebedo recommends the following elements of principled negotiation to work through the conflict. These are universal and can be applied to just about any dispute you and your spouse are having—financial or otherwise.

I'm going to walk you through the framework in this chapter so you know what you should be focusing on. Later, in Chapter 9, I'll go over my favorite exercises that help to take the focus off the specific conflict and onto these four elements as a way to help you move forward.

RESOLVING MONEY ARGUMENTS

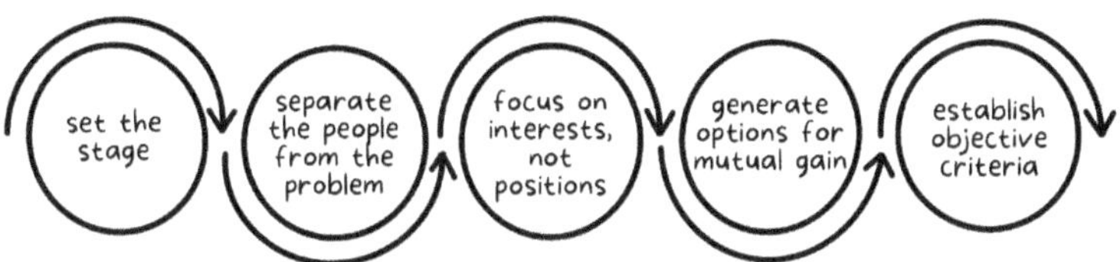

Separate the people from the problem. When you articulate the problem that you're looking to solve, you should always make the problem itself the focal point of the discussion—not your spouse's thoughts or actions.

(Here's a helpful hint: if you find yourself drifting into Four Horsemen territory, you are focusing on your spouse too much and not enough on the problem.)

The first step to solving the conflict is to identify the root cause or specific problem you're facing and agree on what the problem is together. Once you both agree on the problem, you can work together to solve it.

For example, a spouse who says, "You keep running up your credit card balance because you're spending your money irresponsibly, and we don't have enough money to pay it off each month!" is focusing on their spouse, not the problem itself.

A way to reframe this to properly focus on the root problem would be to say something like, "Our income isn't high enough to cover all of our total expenses and credit card bills."

Focus on interests, not positions. Remember, in a Marriage-Centered Financial Plan, money is not the goal or destination of the plan—it's the sail in the sailboat that you use to reach the destination. As such, the financial opinions you have about the conflict should *not* be the focus of your attention in this conversation.

To go back to the credit card example, I wouldn't recommend focusing on the actual credit card balance itself when working to resolve the conflict. Rather, what is the underlying concern of the spouse expressing frustration about the credit card debt? Likely, they want to protect their family's financial security.

By approaching the conversation with the focus on the interest of increasing their family's financial security rather than the credit card debt itself, it puts the focus on the most important things that, more often than not, will appeal to both spouses. It also opens up doors to alternative solutions.

The challenge with this step, though, is that it requires both spouses to be vulnerable and to participate in the conversation in good faith. The money history and money scripts conversations you had are designed to help you both open up to each other about these topics, and they are a great place to start flushing out your shared financial interests as a family.

Generate options for mutual gain. Once you've identified your interests, you can start to approach finding the right solution that doesn't violate the interests you uncovered.

I encourage you to brainstorm here. Try to come up with as many solutions to the problem as possible before you actually pick one. And feel free to be creative! You never know what might come up as part of this conversation.

And remember, when you're brainstorming solutions, focus on the underlying interests you have rather than the positions in the argument. Try to broaden the discussion beyond just the issue at hand. In doing so, you are much more likely to generate ideas that will be mutually beneficial.

Establish objective criteria. Once you generate a list of options, it can be very helpful to have an objective standard in place against which you can judge your solution.

Don't worry about setting objective criteria at the beginning. It's important to brainstorm a list of options before trying to evaluate which is the factually superior choice.

But once you have your options available, you should review the underlying numbers to set an objective standard to evaluate each option's likelihood of success. Depending on the nature of the conflict, you may want to consult a neutral third party to analyze the options from an outside perspective to help you identify the one most likely to allow each of you to achieve your underlying interests in the conflict.

———

So far in Part 2 of this book, you've done a *lot* of foundational work to get you and your spouse communicating effectively about money and prepared yourselves to be more coordinated with the way you manage money together. Working through conflicts as they arise is a critical component of this.

In doing this work, you will approach conflicts with a much better understanding of *why* you disagree. Now, keeping this background knowledge in mind and with empathy for your partner and their underlying interests, it's time to follow this process to start working through your financial conflicts.

Be patient, give it time, and don't be afraid to loop in a professional counselor, financial planner, or mediator if you need help.

We're going to take a brief pause in the next chapter to review some warning signs to look out for as you have these conversations. But immediately after, I'm going to show you my favorite tactical way to help your family work through conflicts by separating the people from the problem, focusing on the interests at hand rather than the positions, generating options for mutual gain, and establishing objective criteria in Chapters 9 and 10. If you read the conflict resolution framework in this chapter and thought, "that sounds great, but I don't know where to begin," then you're in luck—just keep reading!

CHAPTER 8

Red Flags

Over the previous few chapters, we've come a long way in exploring the way you and your spouse view money, understanding your financial differences, and working to resolve these conflicts. Before we move on to actually building a forward-looking Marriage-Centered Financial Plan, I wanted to quickly pause to talk about some of the more extreme cases of financially problematic behavior in marriages that I've seen in my work over the years.

This is very intentionally the shortest chapter in this book. No stories, no tactics to use—just the information you need to know to recognize certain situations when you see them and what to do when you find these types of issues.

The ironic part about this being the shortest chapter in the book is that it's also the chapter with the most serious implications.

It's important to recognize when financial differences and financial conflicts go from normal challenges to work through in your marriage to critical threats that need intervention. In the same way that "overspending" is a challenge you can troubleshoot on your own, but "overspending due to a drug addiction" is something requiring professional care to handle appropriately, there are certain financial issues that affect couples that should *not* be addressed in the framework of a Marriage-Centered Financial Plan.

The goal of this chapter isn't to give you step-by-step instructions on how to handle these issues but rather to help you recognize them when you see them so that you can get the appropriate help you need. Each of these items is out of scope in a Marriage-Centered Financial Plan, and if you're struggling with any of these items, it's time to seek one-on-one counseling with an appropriate provider.

Whenever you see the characteristics described in this chapter, you should treat these as "red flag" issues and seek the help of a financial therapist, mental health professional, or marriage counselor. At the end of the day, none of these items are really financial issues at all, even if they manifest themselves in financial topics or discussions.

FINANCIAL ENMESHMENT: IMPROPER FINANCIAL BOUNDARIES

Enmeshment is a concept in the mental health world that describes a relationship where boundaries with others are unclear, in the wrong place, or nonexistent.

In the context of marriage and money, financial enmeshment deals with improper financial boundaries.

Improper boundaries can take many forms. Financial enmeshment can describe unclear or poor boundaries between you and your spouse as individuals or between you and your spouse and other family members.

The most common types of financial enmeshment boundary issues that arise take one of three forms:

Boundary issues between you and your spouse: On one end of the spectrum, this could involve overly rigid financial boundaries between you and your spouse, where you don't share any financial information with the other. On the other end of the spectrum, your family's boundaries could be so blurred that it leads to a culture of financial dependence between the spouses (where, for example, a non-working spouse might become completely dependent on a working spouse in an unhealthy way).

Boundary issues between your immediate family (i.e., you and your spouse) and your parents/in-laws: For example, financial enmeshment issues with your parents might look like a father who wants a say in managing your family's financial investments because he started an investment account (that you still have today) for you when you were a child. Even though you are married now, he might view it as his role and responsibility to see to your financial affairs in managing the money he gave you as a child, even though this will create relationship challenges with you and your spouse.

Boundary issues between you and your children: Generally, your children should not be involved with the way you manage money as a family. There are many ways this boundary can be broken, ranging from a spouse using money to exert influence or control over a child, to sharing too much financial information with a child, to borrowing your child's money for your own purposes, to asking your child to have inappropriate financial duties, to having your child mediate financial disputes with your spouse. All of these behaviors are problematic and should be avoided.

FINANCIAL ENMESHMENT, EXPLAINED

Example 1: (The ideal case) Husband and wife have healthy money boundaries (indicated by the circle in the illustration). They discuss money with each other openly and make financial decisions together and leave their parents and their children out of their finances. There is no financial enmeshment in this scenario.

Example 2: Husband and wife have improper financial boundaries with each other. They do not communicate effectively about money issues. These rigid boundaries are an example of financial enmeshment.

Example 3: Husband and wife communicate effectively about money with each other, but their parents/in-laws are too involved in their financial decision-making. There is an improper boundary between the couple and their parents/in-laws that is drawn in the wrong place. This is an example of financial enmeshment.

Example 4: Husband and wife involve their children in the family's financial decisions or overshare financial details with children at an inappropriate age. There is an improper boundary between the couple and their children that is drawn in the wrong place. This is an example of financial enmeshment.

Regardless of the relationships of the people involved, boundary issues in financial enmeshment can take a few different forms, as you may have observed in the examples above:

Boundaries may be unclear: either because they aren't consistently enforced in the same spots, or they just don't exist at all.

Boundaries may be unhealthy: either because they are too rigid or too flexible.

Boundaries may be drawn incorrectly: i.e., you might have good boundaries in place, but they are drawn in the wrong spot. (This one is the least clear of the three conceptually, so here's an example: you have healthy conversations about money in your family, but they often happen in front of your young children rather than when you and your spouse are alone.)

The lists and examples provided in this section are not meant to be exhaustive. If you suspect that your family has unhealthy boundaries around your finances in any capacity, it's time to reach out to a therapist or marriage counselor to get professional guidance on how to handle setting and enforcing proper boundaries. These sorts of boundary issues put incredible amounts of strain on relationships over time, so it's important to work through these issues before they threaten the foundation of your marriage.

FINANCIAL INFIDELITY: FINANCIAL SECRECY

Usually, we use the word "infidelity" when discussing someone who cheats on their significant other, whether that be physically or emotionally. Financial infidelity doesn't *literally* involve cheating, but it involves the same sense of secrecy.

Financial infidelity involves engaging in any financial behavior that is expected to be disapproved of by one's romantic partner and intentionally failing to disclose this behavior to them. This can take many different forms, and some of the most common include:

- Having credit cards, credit card balances, or other types of debts that you've hidden from your spouse.

- Having bank accounts, investments, or other financial assets that you've hidden from your spouse.

- Keeping income or bonuses secret from your spouse.

- Secretly giving your family's money to causes or people that your spouse would not consent to give money to.

- Gambling your family's money without telling your spouse.

- Filing for bankruptcy without your spouse's knowledge.

Obviously, the context of these things matters. In the same way that one family might not consider flirting with a work colleague a case of marital infidelity, you might not consider some of the examples on the list above to be financial infidelity.

The clearest objective sign that something is an act of financial infidelity, though, is if one spouse is intentionally hiding the action or keeping it secret.

Financial infidelity occurs more commonly than you might expect. A study conducted by researchers at the University of Southern Mississippi in 2018, subsequently published in the Journal of Financial Therapy, found that 27% of people admitted to keeping a financial secret from their partner, and 53% of people reported behaviors associated with financial infidelity. (The difference between those figures suggests a certain level of denial about the degree to which financial secrecy is a problem in marriages. So, before you dismiss this section as not applying to your family, take a moment to check yourself!)

Left unresolved, financial infidelity can create severe trust issues in a marriage and often can have similar emotional effects as physical or emotional infidelity. If you are currently hiding a financial secret from your spouse, or if you have in the past, I highly recommend working with a marriage counselor to unpack this issue, clear the air, and create a path to move your family forward.

FINANCIAL ABUSE: USING MONEY TO CONTROL

Financial abuse, sometimes called economic abuse, occurs when a spouse has control over the other spouse's access to financial and economic resources, which diminishes the victim's capacity to support themselves and forces them to depend on the other person financially.

Financial abuse can include activity that is overtly illegal (such as theft or fraud) or improper behavior that creates situations of financial control within a marriage. It can also include any form of financial pressure designed to cause (or maintain) power differentials in a relationship.

Financial abuse can take many forms. Some specific examples include a spouse:

- Taking money from you without your knowledge.

- Preventing you from going to work or looking for a job.

- Preventing you from having money of your own.

- Demanding to know how money was spent or trying to control how you spend money.

- Limiting your access to money or making you ask them for money.

If you, or someone you know, is a victim of financial abuse, you should immediately seek the help of a family member, friend, mental health professional, or law enforcement.

One final note: Financial abuse doesn't need to be happening right now in your marriage to have an impact on you or your spouse. If any of these things ever happened to you as a child or earlier in your life, you should see a counselor to work through the trauma you experienced related to this abuse.

———

Financial enmeshment, financial infidelity, and financial abuse are three of the most common "red flag" issues that come up in the field of money and marriage. Hopefully, this short chapter helped you recognize the signs of problematic or abusive financial behavior.

Again, if you or your spouse are experiencing (or have experienced in the past) any of these red flags, I recommend putting down this book and getting the appropriate professional help to aid your navigation of these issues and work through them.

PART 3

IMPLEMENTING A MARRIAGE-CENTERED FINANCIAL PLAN

Okay—*now* it's time to talk about your money. In Part 3, we're going to build the "Financial Plan" part of your Marriage-Centered Financial Plan, focusing on the principles of confidence, coordination, clarity, and commitment.

Unlike Part 2, in which some chapters were probably more relevant to your marriage than others, everything in Part 3 is applicable to *everyone*. Each chapter builds off the chapter before it, so you and your spouse should work through this content in order.

We start off with *the* single most important part of your financial plan in Chapter 9, followed by a discussion around setting financial goals in Chapter 10.

Chapter 11 will help you and your spouse identify the right way to set up your financial accounts based on your goals, your financial differences, and your money scripts.

Chapters 12, 13, and 14 cover the four critical areas you and your spouse *must* get on the same page about—budgeting, debt, career decisions, and location—and will show you how to do so.

In Chapter 15, I'll show you my favorite and most successful strategy to help couples maintain momentum in achieving their goals.

And finally, Chapter 16 will cover two seemingly contradictory elements of your financial plan—financial security and financial freedom—and show you how to balance both of these important concepts.

This is the same process I use with my financial planning clients, and it gets great results.

Finally, please remember to keep the information you learned about you and your spouse in Part 2 in mind as you complete each chapter. You've learned the skills you need to handle any financial differences or conflicts that arise as you build your plan. And hopefully, the process you've followed to get to this point will make it less likely that you'll have disagreements along the way!

CHAPTER 9

Mission Statement

I want you to close your eyes for a second and picture your favorite company in the world.

What's a company whose products or services you can't imagine living without?

For me, I can't imagine a world where my day doesn't start with Dunkin Donuts coffee. (What can I say, I might be a DC resident at heart, but my Massachusetts roots run deep!)

I want you to pretend you are in charge of making financial decisions at your chosen company. Your employees come to you with two new product ideas. Both are great ideas on paper, but due to a lack of funds available, you can only choose one.

How do you make this decision?

By reminding yourself what the company's all about in the first place. By focusing on what the company is best at and what's most important to the company. When your values are clear, your decision is easy.

In other words, you would review the company's *mission statement*, which will usually make the investment decision crystal clear.

If you review Dunkin's mission statement (at least as of the time of this writing), you'll notice there is a heavy focus on providing top-quality food and beverages with *speed* and *efficiency*.

Dunkin Donuts is all about providing a consistent product efficiently, so you can get where you need to go. They don't want you to spend your day sitting in their store—they want you to come in, get what you need, and go about your business. (When was the last time you sat in a Dunkin Donuts and read the newspaper or answered some emails? Exactly.)

If you're the head of Dunkin, and you need to figure out what new products or services to offer, you choose the option that's in line with those values. *Anything* else is the wrong option for this specific company.

Now, let's compare this to their biggest competitor, Starbucks.

When you go into a Starbucks, there is a heavy emphasis on the experience you have when you're there. From the ambiance to the music, to the customized drink order, to the names they have for their drink sizes, to the table seating—everything at Starbucks is about the experience, not efficiency.

Of course, all of that is reflected in the company mission statement, which, as of this writing, focuses on providing *nurture* and *inspiration* to its patrons.

Starbucks' mission statement has a *very* different tone and feel than Dunkin's. And this is reflected by the differences in experiences you have when you visit each of them.

The "right" new product idea for Starbucks should look very different than the "right" new product idea for Dunkin. The only reason each company knows which new product to choose is because they took the time to articulate what's most important to them in the form of their mission statements.

Now, what does any of this have to do with Marriage-Centered Financial Planning?

Well, let me answer that question by asking you another. What's *your family's* mission statement?

We've talked about how Dunkin Donuts and Starbucks make financial decisions. It's not just about the numbers—*it's about prioritizing what's most important to them.* You need to do the same thing with your finances. But you can't prioritize the most important things until you identify what those are in the first place.

Have you taken the time to clearly identify what's most important to you and your partner? Have you ever spent twenty to thirty
minutes defining what "success" looks like for your family?

If you have—that's *awesome.* You are one of the rare few.

If not, then now's the time to do so. This is the most important
step to making good financial decisions as a family, and it's one that
most couples overlook.

The right financial decision for you and your spouse is the *wrong*
decision for a lot of other couples.

I've seen people make the wrong career moves, buy the wrong
house, invest in the wrong type of accounts, settle down in the wrong
part of the country—the list goes on and on. Almost always, the
thing that was missing in the decision-making process was a mission statement.

Before I show you *how* you can implement something like this in
your life, go back to the company you love that you identified at the
beginning of the chapter. Look up their mission statement. Think
about how you see this mission statement manifest in the products
and services they create.

Now, let's talk about how you can do the same in your family.

HOW TO KNOW WHAT YOU
REALLY WANT OUT OF LIFE

Completing a family mission statement sounds like it might be
a very broad, unspecific activity. And to some degree, it *is* broad. At
the end of the day, your family mission statement can be whatever
you want it to be.

Generally, I recommend that your family's mission statement con-
sist of a few bullet points summarizing what means most to you as
a family.

I don't want you to start with a blank slate and try to make it up
as you go. So, to help draft these bullet points, I've compiled two different exercises from thought leaders in the financial planning arena
to help guide you and your spouse through this process. You don't

necessarily need to complete them both. In my experience, most couples tend to gravitate toward one exercise rather than the other. But, by completing one or both of these, you'll be well on your way to implementing a powerful family mission statement to guide your future financial decision-making.

Exercise One: The "Carl Richards Question"

As the name implies, I've adapted this first exercise from personal finance expert and New York Times money columnist Carl Richards. The exercise—at least on its surface—only involves answering one specific question:

Why is money important to you?

It's a pretty straightforward question, but there's a catch. I need you to get as specific as possible with your answer.

I ask this in all of my new client meetings, and 99% of the time, the client will answer with one of the following words: "Independence," "Freedom," or "Security." These are qualities *everyone* wants. They are also qualities that are thoroughly meaningless unless you can clearly define them for yourself.

So, if you answered with any of these words, you need to ask yourself a second question: "Why?"

Why do you want to feel more secure, free, independent, or whatever your answer to the first question was? *Why* are those things important to you? And *why* does money make you feel more secure, free, etc.?

It's not enough to ask yourself *why* money is important to you. You need to ask some further questions to get as much clarity on the subject as possible.

You say that money is important to you because it's a source of security? Why does money make you feel secure? Why is *that* something that's important to you? When you've answered that question, ask yourself "why" again. And again. And again. You'll know you're ready to stop when you've reached something incredibly powerful— something that makes you pause for a moment and say "wow" to yourself. And once you've reached that point, ask yourself "why" one more time. I sometimes find that pushing yourself just one more time can make all the difference in the power of what you discover about yourself by doing this exercise.

I find that this exercise is the most powerful place to start when figuring out what it is you want to do with your money. Until we get clear on exactly *why* money is important to you, we can't possibly make good, informed decisions about how you should be saving and spending your money.

Exercise Two: The "George Kinder Questions"

I've experimented with numerous strategies and exercises over the years to help clients create their family mission statement. And there's nothing—*nothing*—out there that works better than a set of three questions developed by financial planning pioneer George Kinder.

Whenever I get the sense that someone isn't quite sure what it is they want out of their lives—or even more importantly, when someone immediately tells me what they want to accomplish, but I get the feeling that there's something deeper they are overlooking—these three questions come out. And they've never failed me at getting to the heart of the issue.

Again, full credit for this exercise goes to George Kinder at the Kinder Institute of Life Planning. I've seen this exercise change the entire trajectory of people's lives, and I hope you find it as powerful as I do.

I've briefly summarized each of Kinder's questions below. I encourage you to review the full version of each question at the Kinder Institute of Life Planning's website when completing your family's mission statement.

Question One: Imagine you won the lottery and no longer need to worry about money. What would you do, and what would you change?

Question Two: Imagine you went to the doctor and learned you only have five to ten years left to live. What would you do with the time you have left?[2]

Question Three: Imagine you learned that you only had one day left to live. The question is *not* what would you do with the day you had left. But rather, what did you miss out on in life? What did you not get to do or be?

As you think through your answers to these questions, there are a few things you should look for:

Are there any commonalities between your answers? If there are items that show up in your answers to each of the three questions, take a second and highlight those items however you can. These are items we need to address as soon as possible. Any decisions you make around how to use your money need to be directed at rectifying these items.

Are there things that show up in question one that don't show up in the later questions? These sorts of items are also important to note but, by definition, are less important than your answers to questions two and three. We should still keep these items in mind when we create your financial goals, but they should be secondary.

It probably goes without saying, but the answers to question three are the most important. In many ways, the point of working through questions one and two are to get you in the right frame of mind to answer question three freely and openly. And in my opinion, your mission statement *must* address each of the items that come up in question three.

In my experience in coaching couples through these three questions, and based on Mr. Kinder's research, several common items

---

2. These questions don't build on one another. So, for question one, you have all the money you could ever need, but this is not the case for questions two and three.

tend to come up in question three. You may have come up with several of these, or only one, or maybe even a completely different list entirely. But the most common items or regrets are:

- Family and/or relationships: These types of regrets can take many forms—spending more time with family, repairing fractured or dormant relationships, regrets about not having children, and more. These sorts of items don't come up for everyone, but they are typically the most common and the strongest when they *do* occur. As we consider the financial changes you are looking to make in your life, we need to take these items into account.

- Place: Location is another common item that comes up. Maybe you live in the middle of a big city for your job, but you've always dreamed about living in the mountains somewhere. Or maybe you've always intended to move back to the city where you grew up, but the timing hasn't worked out. Another common item that comes up here is wanting to have a home of your own. These items aren't always *directly* related to your finances, but they all have financial implications that we need to address. (We're going to revisit this question in Chapter 14.)

- Values: Living a life that's not in line with your values is exceptionally common, particularly in our generation. Sometimes, this can be explicitly spiritual or religious in nature, but more often, these sorts of regrets pop up when you aren't passionate about what you're doing with your life. And sometimes, our work or how we spend our free time directly contradicts what we say is important to us. If this is you, I can relate. The good news is that the rest of this book is focused on correcting this misalignment and bringing your life back in line with what's important to you.

- Freedom and creativity: This category is something of a catch-all for items that arise in question three relating to a lack of fulfillment. Maybe you've always wanted to have a particular experience or participate in a particular hobby, or even start a business. Unless we intentionally prioritize these sorts of creative activities, they tend to get swept under the rug. If this applies to you, we will focus on some strategies to help you make a change.

- Making a difference: It's very common for regrets to surface relating to giving back to society. Some people wish they were able to give more of their time or treasure to particular causes. Whether your version of philanthropy involves giving money to a cause, volunteering, or even making a living by supporting such causes, it's critical that your financial plan addresses these areas that are important to you.

- Travel/experiences: This one is much more common in answers to questions one and two. Having particular life experiences, including travel, is another common item to work into your financial plan.

We are going to revisit many of the items on the above list in subsequent chapters.

Again, the items that surfaced for you might look completely different from this list. Your list should be unique to you. Either way, you should pay careful attention to the matters that arose as you completed the exercises in this chapter.

PUTTING IT ALL TOGETHER: YOUR FAMILY FINANCIAL MISSION STATEMENT

You've now completed two exercises—the "Carl Richards Question" (and subsequent probing) and the three "Kinder Questions"— that are designed to help you identify what's *really* important to you in your lives. The final step is to merge all of the things that came up for you while going through these exercises. The final product is a family mission statement that we will use to guide all of your financial decisions going forward.

Go back to your notes from these two exercises. Consolidate your notes into two or three bullet points that summarize, as completely as possible, the items that are most important to you as you've identified them. Your list can be longer than two or three bullet points, but make sure it's focused on the most critical things that came up during these exercises.

Here's an example of what this looks like in practice: I once worked with a newlywed couple, who we will call Jen and James. Jen and James had good jobs that they enjoyed, but they were both miserably unhappy with where they lived. The question they came to me to discuss was how to move to a completely new location and make it work financially while both would be changing jobs.

Seems pretty straightforward, right?

Not quite.

The first complicating factor was that neither of them *really* wanted to leave their jobs. They weren't happy with where they were living, but they were happy with their work, and they were both anxious about giving that component up.

So, that's when I decided to ask the three Kinder questions.

Question One: What would you do if you won the lottery?

James said, "I'd quit my job." Jen agreed.

Their current jobs *felt* really important to them, but when given the opportunity to stop working, they both took it immediately. Right away, that showed me that in the decision between staying in a place they hated and keeping the jobs they loved, moving to a new location was going to be the winner.

I then continued with the second question, which puts an intermediate time limit on their lives. I heard a similar answer here. They both hoped they would want to minimize their work time and be bolder with how they were living their lives. Spending more time with family also cropped up in their answers to question two, as it often does.

But then I dropped the third question on them. What would they have missed in their lives if they only had twenty-four hours left to live? This is where things got interesting quickly. This is a heavy question that often invokes strong emotions. And this case was no different.

Both Jen and James started by citing relationships that had lapsed. They wished for the opportunity to reconnect with old friends and some family members they used to see when they were growing up but had lost touch with lately.

But then, Jen paused and burst into tears (which is not uncommon in this exercise). She paused and said, "I'd really regret that I never had the chance to be a mom. We haven't wanted to start a family until we live in a more family-friendly community, a town where we can envision raising our children. I'd really regret not doing that."

Bingo.

The conversation began by discussing whether it made sense for them to leave jobs they liked to move to a new location. And it ended by recognizing they absolutely *had* to move, quickly, in order to live a life wholly in line with what's important to them as a family. Suddenly, moving to a new place wasn't a question to consider financially—it was a *necessity*, and my job became wholly focused on helping them use their money to achieve this goal.

After going through this exercise with the client, I drafted their family mission statement. It looked something like this:

SAMPLE MISSION STATEMENT

✓ Being grounded in a family-friendly community that feels like home

✓ Growing our family

FINANCIAL CONFLICT RESOLUTION AND MISSION STATEMENTS

When creating your family's financial mission statement, it's important for you each to complete the two exercises on your own at first.

Why? It's important that both of you have an equal voice, especially for exercises as weighty as these. Remember what we discussed a few chapters back about setting the stage for financial conflict resolution? One of the most important steps in handling conflict as a family is to balance power. By starting these exercises individually, you can make sure that both of your perspectives are heard.

Once you each have drafted your answers separately, you should then share your results and use *both* of your statements to draft your mission statement. Your family's financial mission statement should reflect *both* of you equally.

It's common for some disagreements to pop up here. And that's absolutely 100% okay and normal. Use this exercise as a chance to talk some of these things out with your partner and find a way to make this work for both of you.

Back in Chapter 7, I mentioned that the family mission statement was one of my favorite tools to use to help couples handle financial conflict, and that's because it arguably addresses all four key elements in the framework for resolving money arguments:

Separate the People from the Problem: The mission statement is designed to shift your thinking from the specific disputes you are having with your spouse to your most important values and the challenges you are having in your life. There is zero reason to fight with your spouse when developing a mission statement since you are moving beyond the day-to-day frustrations that sometimes develop in your marriage and focusing on the dreams for your future instead.

Focus on Interests, Not Positions: There are no "positions" in a mission statement. By definition, you aren't picking sides when completing these exercises. Instead, the mission statement exercises are designed to get you and your spouse dreaming about your future together.

Generate Options for Mutual Gain: The mission statement is developed by you and your spouse as a team, which means the mission statement as a whole should represent both of your shared perspectives. And the mission statement itself isn't prescriptive—there are a *lot* of different financial tools, tactics, and strategies you can use to realize the vision you create for yourselves. Because it is an aspirational standard, it intentionally allows you flexibility in the vehicles you use to fulfill the mission statement, which in turn allows you and your spouse to brainstorm creative options on how to proceed.

Establish Objective Criteria: You might argue that your family's mission statement isn't "objective" in the sense that you both developed it based on your subjective preferences, but I think that misses the point. The mission statement is something you both agreed should be your guiding star in financial decision-making. So, whenever you need to make a difficult financial decision or are having a financial conflict, you can use the mission statement as the objective standard to determine the right option going forward.

That's the beauty of the family mission statement. By learning to focus on the right things, you will reduce the frequency of day-to-day arguments about money, and when they do arise, they become much easier to handle.

———

Now, it's your turn. Go back through your answers to the exercises in this chapter and come up with a few bullet points that touch on the most important items to you. These bullet points *need to be* your guiding star when it comes to your finances. Everything else will fall into place around them. It might take some time, but starting today, this is what we are going to focus your finances on.

CHAPTER 10

Goal Setting

The typical human being can endure up to four seconds of awkward silence in a conversation before they feel compelled to say something to fill the gap. In September of 2020, I learned that I was capable of waiting a *lot* longer.

The specific incident occurred about five minutes into my first conversation with Carly and Chris. They came to me asking the types of questions that most people think they're supposed to ask a financial planner—they had a ton of different scattered investment accounts and wanted to make sure the investments they had in these accounts were good ones.

I smiled to myself, knowing I was about to enforce one of my self-developed Principles of Financial Planning.[3]

You see, everyone *thinks* they should reach out to financial planners and focus on investment decisions. But, according to Nelson's 3rd Principle of Financial Planning, "Nobody *really* cares about investments; *everyone* cares about what their investments enable them to do."

And so, when Chris and Carly began our conversation with talk

---

3. Much in the spirit of Newton's 3 Laws of Gravity, I've developed similar principles of financial planning over the years. One of which is the premise behind this book: "Managed properly, money can strengthen your marriage." Another is, "The more complex an investment is, the worse it is for the average investor." And so on. Maybe I'll create a book of all of these laws someday; you'll just have to wait and see!

of their investment portfolio, I knew they weren't *really* here to talk about setting up their investment accounts. They were here to talk about what they wanted those investment accounts to do for them and then, in turn, to make sure they were calibrated appropriately to help them achieve these goals.

And so, I asked the question that prompted no less than thirty seconds of the most excruciating, enjoyable silence I've ever had the privilege of participating in:

"So, the money you have in these investment accounts that you mentioned. What do you want to use it for?"

Now, in the last chapter, you got to experience some of the weighty questions I ask couples—questions about life and death. As you might imagine, I've gotten a variety of responses to these types of questions over the years.

But never—NEVER—have I been met by such a long, profound silence as I was when I asked Chris and Carly what they wanted to use their money for.

They were completely stuck. They were so focused on the money at hand that they never stopped to consider what the money was actually for, and they essentially told me as such when they finally broke the silence.

"We mostly just wanted to make sure the accounts were growing. I hadn't really thought about what we'd use the money for," Chris finally replied.

"Obviously, the retirement accounts are for retirement," Carly added. "But I have no idea what we'd do with the rest of it."

Fast forward a few months later, and things looked completely different.

Obviously, I helped Chris and Carly do what they came to me for—we consolidated some of their accounts and tweaked their investment approach in each account as needed.

But the biggest benefit they got from the experience was clarity on where their money was today and, more importantly, where their money was taking them.

I helped them set concrete goals about retirement, buying a

vacation or rental property, and giving back to a few environmental non-profit agencies that they really cared about (which was directly inspired by their family's new mission statement). From there, we aligned their investment accounts to directly support these goals, and we made sure they were invested appropriately to give them the best possible chance of success.

In short: we didn't "just" focus on their investments. We first got clear on their goals and then created an investment game plan for how to achieve these goals.

TRANSLATING YOUR FAMILY MISSION STATEMENT TO TANGIBLE GOALS

In the last chapter, we talked a lot about how you want to be living your life. We talked about your deepest and most important values and the degree to which you are (or are not) living out this vision for your dream life right now.

What we haven't done—at least not yet—is talk about your money. And specifically, how to use your money to live out this mission. That changes now.

It's time to turn your family's mission statement into tangible, actionable financial goals.

It's time to go from a line item in your mission statement like "Being grounded in a family-friendly community that feels like home" to a goal like "Buy a four-bedroom home in Loudoun County, Virginia, for $350,000 in one year with a 20% down payment."

If you recall the story of Jen and James from Chapter 9, this particular example was predicated on a couple who wanted to move to a family-friendly community so they could grow their family. Their vision was to live in an environment where they would be able to raise kids with the "right" values and in the "right" community for them.

Is this a great vision? Absolutely. (At least, it was for Jen and James. Your mission statement can and *should* be different!) Is it something that's actionable or tangible? Not quite.

However, the goal I mentioned above is *incredibly* specific. We've gone from a broad, overall picture to something we can hold our-selves to. It's very hard for someone to know whether they are actually "grounded" in a "family-friendly" community that "feels like home." But, as long as the goal is in line with this vision, it's *very* easy to track progress against the goal. This goal is so specific that we can measure:

- The amount of money they need to finance this goal: $70,000 (20% of $350,000).

- When they need the money: a year from today.

- What they are looking for: the house isn't just a "house." Since they were looking to expand their family, they want to buy a four-bedroom house.

- Where they want to buy: Loudoun County, VA—about a half-hour outside Washington, DC.

This is the process that will take you from your overarching mission statement for your family to the specific actions you need to take in order to recognize this vision. By setting tangible, actionable financial goals and monitoring your progress in achieving them, you will move yourselves toward your dream lives.

HOW SPECIFIC SHOULD YOUR GOALS BE?

The house in Loudoun County in the previous example was *very* specific. Do all of your goals need to be this way?

In an ideal world, they perhaps should be. If we want your Marriage-Centered Financial Plan to be as accurate as possible, it would be nice to make sure the goals are specific enough that you don't accidentally miss the mark!

Here's the problem with setting such specific goals, though: it's *really* hard to be so specific in what you want decades into the future, which makes it hard to be especially precise with your long-term goals.

So, as a general rule of thumb: the closer you are to achieving the goal, the more specific your goal should be.

If you're looking to buy a house in the next year or two, you *should* push yourselves to be as specific as "Buy a four-bedroom home in Loudoun County, VA, for $350,000 in one year with a 20% down payment." But if you're in the first half of your career, something like your retirement goal can be vaguer.

In fact, I'd argue that "Fully fund our 401(k)s each year" is a *much* better goal for a thirty-year-old than "Save $2,367,927 for retirement by the time we are sixty-seven years old." It's hard to know whether you're on track for the latter, but it's much easier to monitor the former!

Even for shorter-term goals, I often find that people are hesitant to get specific because most of us are afraid to commit to what we will want in the future.

None of us *actually* know exactly what we want our future to look like. Life doesn't work that way. If you're looking at the example of the $350,000 house and thinking to yourself, "How in the world am I supposed to know how expensive of a house I want to buy, when I want to buy it, and where I want to buy it?" then I'll say it once again—this is a completely normal feeling to have this early in the process. The vast majority of people don't map out their lives that way.

I always struggled with how to help couples bridge this gap until I heard Carl Richards (of "The Carl Richards Question" fame from Chapter 9) describe financial goals as your "best guess" about the future. According to Richards, you might not know the specifics with 100% confidence. Or 75% confidence. Or even less.

But you know enough to make a guess. And making a guess is enough ... at least for now!

In this spirit, when setting specific financial goals, you should think of your goals as "best guess" goals or "almost final draft" goals. They won't be perfect, and they don't need to be. But they will give you something to work toward and a way to measure your progress.

To go back to the Loudoun County house goal example, there are *so many* things that could change over time that would require this goal to need some updates.

What if the house we buy ends up being $400,000? What if four bedrooms aren't the right number of bedrooms? What if property values in Loudoun County skyrocket, and we will no longer be able to afford to buy a house there?

None of that matters for now. Do your best to set the most accurate goal possible and start working toward it.

Your goals can—and will—change over time. But at the very least, they'll give you a target to shoot for. You can always tweak them as you go.

GOALS TO INCLUDE IN YOUR MARRIAGE-CENTERED FINANCIAL PLAN

"Goals" is a very open-ended word. When we talk about adding goals to your plan, what should these goals look like?

I'll give you some specific examples in a moment, but I actually find that the clearest way to think about your financial goals is through the lens of the mission statement you developed in Chapter 9.

Your mission statement consists of a series of bullet points that reflect what you and your spouse want for your family. Each of the items in your mission statement is intangible and aspirational.

The job of your financial goals is to take each of the bullet points in your mission statement and translate them into *actionable* items.

Each portion of your family's mission statement should have one or more goals that will help you and your spouse bring this mission statement into reality. And on the flip side, if a goal that either of you is considering isn't in line with your mission statement, it's probably the wrong goal for your family.

By using your mission statement as the starting point, you can be sure you are setting the right financial goals for your family.

That being said, financial goals often fall into certain categories. So, if you need help getting started, use the following list for inspiration:

SAMPLE FINANCIAL GOAL CATEGORIES

√ Paying down debt

√ Establishing and maintaining an emergency fund

√ Charitable giving

√ Preparing for retirement

√ Buying a house or maintaining a house

√ Big-ticket purchases: cars, boats, vacation homes, etc.

√ Saving for college

√ Leaving a legacy—to your family or a specific cause

√ Income and career changes

√ Starting a business

Finally, don't be afraid to get creative with your goals! I know a couple who made it their goal to save >80% of their salary every year until they were thirty-five and then completely retire in their mid-thirties. On the flip side, I know of a few couples who took the completely opposite approach, setting their work up to be exceptionally flexible with reduced hours, so they had enough time to live the life of their dreams now and never even *want* to retire.

One of my good friends has highly specialized knowledge about sustainable food systems. She has formal education in the field, and she set a goal to open up a sustainable farm and bakery.

But she recognized that to accomplish this, she needed some hands-on experience working in a few different capacities in the farming and food industries. So, she got creative and set some goals to leave her full-time job, do some food sustainability consulting to support herself, and work part-time in a bakery and as a laborer on a farm to get the experience she needed to achieve her long-term business goals.

These goals fall well outside of the "standard" financial planning goals you would typically think of. But they are great examples of setting goals in line with your vision for the future.

At the end of the day, your goals can be whatever you want them to be, as long as they support your family's mission statement and you and your spouse are in agreement.

TRACKING YOUR GOALS

Once you've identified your financial goals, the final piece is to figure out how you're going to achieve them.

For each goal, I recommend identifying and writing down the following:

- What is the goal that you're setting? This should be in line with everything we've covered in this chapter up until this point.

- How much do you need to set aside to achieve the goal? (E.g., $24,000 for a used car.)

- What's the target date to achieve this goal? (E.g., In two years.)

- How much do you need to set aside per month to achieve this goal? (E.g., $1,000 per month.)

Complete this exercise for each of the goals you identified in this chapter. You should end up with a list of how much money you want to direct toward each of these goals on a monthly or annual basis.

In Chapter 12, we will go through the process of setting a budget to determine how much you can realistically set aside each month to fund your goals. If the total amount you need for each of your goals is reasonable based on your budget, you don't need to do anything else (other than, of course, actually saving the money!)

If you *don't* think you'll be able to save for all of your goals at once, though, there are a few things you can consider doing:

Prioritize your goals based on your mission statement. Some of your goals are likely non-negotiable in that they are critical to achieving the vision you created in your mission statement, but others might be more "wants" than "needs." If you can temporarily pause some of the more discretionary goals to focus on the most critical ones for now, this is the first thing you should consider doing.

Consider focusing on one goal at a time. By directing your focus on one goal at a time, you might be surprised at how quickly you can generate momentum for yourselves. Just like when you're trying to be productive at work, you tend to get more done by focusing on one thing rather than multitasking—the same thing happens when you focus on improving your finances. By focusing on one thing at a time, you are likely to make faster progress than you would otherwise.

Adjust your spending. If there's room in your budget to shift some of your spending until you achieve one or two of the goals, then go for it ... but be careful not to be unrealistic about how much you can cut from your budget for months or years at a time.

SET YOUR FINANCIAL GOALS—TODAY!

We will talk more about how to monitor progress toward your goals in later chapters. For now, it's time to set some specific goals that will help you realize the vision for your life that you created in Chapter 9.

Take some time to translate each bullet point in your mission statement into one (or more!) specific goals. These goals are typically related to your finances, although they may certainly incorporate other areas of your life as well.

If you take anything away from this chapter, know that setting goals that are specific and in line with your mission statement is the best step you can take to improve your life. They don't need to be perfect, and, in fact, they *won't* be perfect. (Remember, we call it "best guess goal setting" for a reason!) But give yourself a target to shoot for. As needed, you can reevaluate and adjust the target along the way.

CHAPTER 11

Account Architecture

The good news for George and Gina was that they had a *lot* of money. The bad news? They didn't know where it was.

When I first met them, they had over $150,000 scattered across *fourteen* different checking and savings accounts.

When I asked them why they had so many different checking and savings accounts, their response might have been more extreme than most couples … but the overall answer was an all too common one.

"Well," George said, "I had three different checking accounts before we got married. One to use for my primary bills, one that was tied to a local credit union where I had my auto loan, and a third at a big national bank that I've had ever since I was a teenager. I also had savings accounts at each of these places, plus a high-yield online savings account I use for most of my savings." And while he didn't actively use most of these accounts on a day-to-day basis, they each had at least $5,000 in them. This meant that it didn't *feel* like he had a ton of cash on hand, but when considering all his accounts together, he really did.

Gina's story was much the same. She "only" had two individual checking accounts, but she had four savings accounts, each of which was set up for various savings goals she's had since she was in college.

Finally, they had one joint checking account that they opened after they moved in together to pay their rent and utilities.

Most of their money was separated, not because they had made the conscious decision not to combine finances, but because they had never gotten around to consolidating accounts and deciding what should be combined and what should stay separate. And there was no rhyme or reason to the accounts they did have. They had slowly added accounts over time out of convenience rather than as a way to help improve their financial standing.

George and Gina came to me, among other reasons, to implement the right financial account structure based on their individual financial habits and attitudes to get them on the same financial page and make it *easy* for them to save money.

And they got there!

We opened a few new accounts, consolidated a lot of others, and streamlined the way they managed money as a family to accelerate their progress. But not before we got really clear on the optimal approach for them to manage money together and intentionally implemented an account structure that reduced the chances of financial conflict in their relationship.

"Should I combine accounts with my spouse?" is one of the most common questions I get from couples, and it's a deceptively tough one to answer.

It's not that there aren't "right" or "wrong" answers to this question. Because there are.

Rather, the right choice depends on how you and your partner interact with money. The "right" choice for one couple could very well be the wrong choice for another.

Most couples come into a marriage with a variety of separate financial accounts. Some couples decide to open new joint accounts. Sometimes, these couples close out the old accounts they aren't using anymore, but more often, old accounts just sit there.

The problem with most of our bank account structures is that they come together piece by piece over time, without a coherent strategy holding all of the accounts together. This is true for individuals, but it's especially true for couples right after getting married. The end result is an account structure that makes it hard to be clear on where your money is today and where your money is going. And in terms of your relationship, a poorly designed financial account structure tends to exacerbate money fights or money avoidance.

You want to set up a financial account structure that a) works for you and your spouse's money scripts and financial differences, and b) is in line with the goals that you've set to make your progress easy to track. Let's tackle each of these pieces one step at a time.

TO COMBINE OR NOT COMBINE...
THAT IS THE QUESTION

When deciding whether you should combine bank accounts with your spouse, you have three choices: combine *nothing*, combine *everything*, and combine *some* things. The right answer for your family largely depends on how you and your spouse manage money together.

Let's consider each option and the pros and cons associated with them, one at a time.

Option 1: Keeping Everything Separate

Going out to eat with one of my groups of friends back in 2013 forever opened my eyes to the different ways that couples manage money together.

There were eight or nine of us total, grabbing dinner at a local brick oven pizza restaurant. We hadn't seen each other in a while, so there was plenty to catch up about. But I remember that the big topic of discussion was the upcoming wedding of two of my friends who were there that night—let's call them Jack and Jill.

Jack and Jill were the first people in the group slated to tie the knot, and we were all looking forward to their wedding in a few months.

Eventually, it came time to pay the bill and head out for the night. And as is common with big groups, we began the process of splitting the tab person by person.

I was sitting next to Jill at the time, and I remember turning to her and saying, "You must be looking forward to doing less of this bill splitting after you get married." (Mind you, this was a few years before I became a financial planner. I'd approach the situation differently now!)

She turned and looked at me, puzzled. "What do you mean?" she asked.

"Well, I'd just imagine it would be easier for you and Jack to handle these sorts of bills after you're married and have combined accounts."

"I'm not sure we're going to do that," she replied. "My parents never combined accounts after they got married and still split everything."

"Really?" I replied, stunned.

"Yeah," she said. "If it worked for them, it would probably work for us."

Jill—and Jill's parents—aren't alone. According to a 2018 Bank of America Study, 28% of millennial couples keep their finances separate after getting married. This rate is higher than in previous generations—the same study showed that 13% of Baby Boomers and 11% of Gen Xers didn't combine finances after getting married.

OPTION 1: KEEP ACCOUNTS SEPARATE

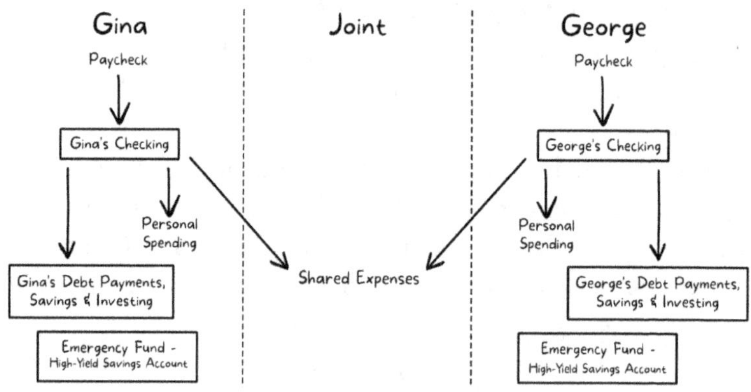

There are a lot of reasons why married partners might choose to keep their finances separate:

Maintaining the status quo. You've managed your money separately up until you get married,[4] and it's worked out so far. Why switch up a strategy that's worked well for you? In this context, leaving your accounts separate after marriage can feel like the most natural approach.

It feels like the safest option. In a world where money is one of the primary causes of divorce, it can sometimes feel safer *not* to combine finances with your spouse. To some couples, this feeling of safety comes from (perceived) legal benefits ("If we end up getting divorced, I'll have all of my money separate to use to rebuild my life."). For others, the safety comes from avoiding rocking the boat ("What if we fight about money more frequently after we combine?"). Money is a really difficult topic for many couples to talk about, and it can feel safer and easier to avoid talking about it altogether. Keeping your finances separate helps to avoid this—or at the very least, it helps to keep money conversations from going too "deep."

Despite this, for almost every couple I've talked with about money in a professional setting, I find that keeping everything separate after getting married is a big mistake. There are a *lot* of reasons why I *do not* recommend couples keep all of their finances separate:

The feeling of safety is an illusion. Keeping your finances separate from your spouse might make you *feel* safer financially, but that doesn't mean that this safety is real. In fact, I'd argue the opposite.

Legally, keeping financial accounts separate will *not* protect you in the event of a divorce, absent a prenup or a postnup (which we will discuss in Chapter 16). The idea that you automatically get to keep your separate accounts if you split up is a myth.

Most states require that assets be divided *fairly* between spouses in the event of a divorce, and this includes separate accounts.

---

4. For a variety of reasons, you *shouldn't* combine accounts until you get legally married. Even if you're engaged or living with a boyfriend or girlfriend, I don't recommend combining accounts until you have a legal framework in place for how to handle them if things in your relationship go south.

And for a handful of states[5] that are classified as "Community Property states," everything you acquired during the marriage (including the separate income that goes into your separate accounts) will be treated as shared property that belongs to both of you.

Whether your accounts are joint or individual doesn't ultimately make a big difference—the state will require you to divide your assets according to its specified framework. Keeping your money separate won't legally protect you.

As far as the safety about not "rocking the boat" is concerned, in my experience, avoiding talking about money is often worse than fighting. These money fights usually aren't about money at all—money is just the way these issues often manifest. By addressing the underlying causes of the money fights, rather than avoiding the discussion by keeping your finances separate, you'll remove roadblocks in your relationship.

What do you want your life to look like fifty years from now? For couples who are making the transition from single life to married life (or who have only been married for a few years), having some degree of fear around combining money is only natural.

It can sometimes be hard to see how combining your finances might be the right decision for your family if managing money separately is all you've ever known.

Still, I find that projecting these decisions out decades into the future can help you see things in a different light and doing so usually convinces couples that keeping their finances completely separate can be a mistake.

Imagine life when you're seventy or eighty years old, retired with your spouse.

Do you still want to be taking the time and energy to split your bills that far down the road?

What if you do a much better job saving for retirement than your

---

5. As of this writing, these states are Arizona, California, Idaho, Louisiana, Nevada, New Mexico, Texas, Washington, and Wisconsin.

spouse? If your spouse can't afford to travel with you during retirement, do you *really* want to stay at home with them (or travel by yourself) just because you decided to always pay your own way?

Usually, when I talk couples through these questions, the answers are immediate. "No, no, Bill," they say, "by that point, it will make sense for us to combine at least some of our accounts."

"What's going to change between now and then?" I typically ask in response. "If now isn't the right time to combine, but there *will* be times in the future when it will make sense, how will you know when you're at the inflection point when it will make sense for you to start combining accounts?"

Usually, the answer to that question is an awkward silence. And typically, most of the objections at this point have to do with some of the safety myths we've already discussed.

You don't need to combine *everything*, as we'll discuss in a bit, but at some point, you're going to want to start combining some things.

Not combining finances can create weird power dynamics in your relationship. This is a big one that I find often goes underappreciated at first, but it can create *big* problems down the road for couples. And once again, it can take a few forms. I find these power dynamics often show up when one spouse doesn't work outside the home or makes (significantly) less money than the other.

If you keep things separate, how do you decide who pays for groceries, childcare, housing, and so on?

Do you split things 50/50, even if there are big income disparities between you and your spouse? If so, this is a really good recipe for feelings of burden and resentment to occur for the partner who has the lower income.

Or do you decide to split everything proportionally? So, if you make 70% of your household income, you decide to pay for 70% of the mortgage, childcare, etc. and have your partner pay for the remaining 30%. Approaching your finances like this is a great way to make the lower-earning spouse feel like he or she has less of a say in financial decisions in your family. It often leads to the higher-earning spouse feeling like they should have control over the major financial decisions your family makes.

What if you decide together that one of you will leave the workforce to become a stay-at-home parent? This can work really well if you have your accounts combined, and a lot of couples make this financial choice for the benefit of their family. But this can become *very* problematic from a relationship power dynamics perspective if you keep your finances separate. (I assure you, getting a personal spending "allowance" from your spouse's separate checking account because you are a stay-at-home parent and don't have an income is a *horrible* thing for your relationship.)

It won't help you grow closer. We've talked a lot about ways in which keeping your finances separate could create rifts in your marriage. But at the end of the day, even if things go *well* for you keeping your finances separate, the best-case scenario is that money won't actively harm your relationship in the process.

Keeping your finances separate definitely won't help you and your spouse grow closer. When you don't *need* to work together financially to solve the problems that life will throw your way, money will only be something that has the potential to drive you and your spouse apart.

Option 2: Combining Everything

"Wait, you share a *VENMO* account with your wife?"

It's been over five years since Mary Kathryn and I decided to combine *literally* all of our finances, right down to our Venmo account. And I still enjoy seeing the reactions from my friends when I send them a Venmo payment from "Mary Kathryn and Bill Nelson."

I'll be the first to acknowledge that combining *Venmo* accounts is pretty extreme. But, for Mary Kathryn and me, it's worked. Remember, Marriage-Centered Financial Planning is all about implementing the right strategies given you and your spouse's different money beliefs, habits, and values. For some couples, combining all your bank accounts is one of the *worst* things you can do. (And that's *completely* okay!) But unlike keeping all your accounts separate, I do recommend to some couples that they combine all their accounts.

OPTION 2: COMBINE EVERYTHING

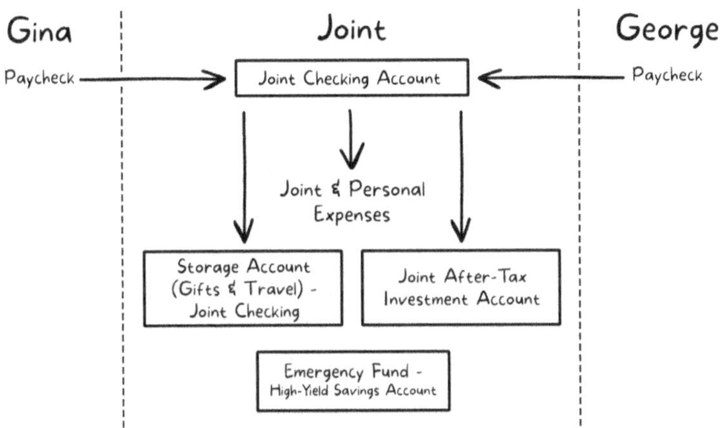

Here are the reasons that Mary Kathryn and I decided to make this choice:

We don't fight about money. I'll come right out and mention this one at the beginning: if money is something you fight about regularly, combining all of your checking accounts and credit cards is the *last* thing you should do. (At least until you implement some of the other strategies in this book to reduce your money fights.)

Particularly for couples who have saver/spender differences, combining your bank accounts can shine a bright spotlight on these differences in a way that will *increase* the frequency of your money fights.

But, if money *isn't* something you fight about regularly, combining your accounts can be a great strategy to help bring you closer to your spouse.

Mary Kathryn and I have certain things we bicker about, as all couples do, but spending generally isn't one of them. In other words, there was no concrete reason that stood out that suggested we *shouldn't* combine accounts.

In fact, we found that the opposite was true for us. For a while, after we got married, and even after we combined checking accounts, Mary Kathryn and I each occasionally used separate credit cards. We quickly found that the financial disagreements we had were coordination issues where one of us would be caught off guard by a particularly high credit card balance on an account we couldn't see.

At the end of the day, we found that it worked better for us to combine everything. So, we did.

It makes it very easy to see our financial progress. From a purely logistical standpoint, combining accounts is often just easier.

How many checking accounts do we have? One. It's *very* easy for us to see exactly how much spending money we have—just log into the (one) bank account, look at the balance, and there it is.

How many savings accounts do we have? Two. One account for our emergency fund and one for our short-term savings goal.[6] It takes us about seventeen seconds to know whether we are on track to reach our goal because everything is in one spot.

By combining our accounts, we are able to easily track our financial progress over time. Each of us can quickly log in to see where we are at and identify if any changes need to be made. We each have access to all of our financial information in a matter of minutes.

Our account structure makes it easy to see if we're on track to reach our financial dreams. The net effect of this hasn't just been to improve our financial situation, but it's also helped to bring us closer together. And on that note…

Combining accounts shows that we're "all in." Combining our finances has been one of the ways that Mary Kathryn and I demonstrate to each other that we aren't holding anything back. That we're in this together. That we're "all in."

To be crystal clear: taking the opposite approach *doesn't* mean you

---

6. My use of the singular tense "goal" here, rather than "goals," is intentional. As we will discuss later in the chapter, I usually recommend having separate accounts for each goal, which means that the second savings account is only used for one goal.

aren't "all in." There are plenty of couples who don't combine their finances and are 100% committed to each other.

But, as my wife and I discussed these issues before we got married, we both decided that combining all of our finances was very important to us. We didn't want to hold anything back from each other—and it's worked out well for us so far.

(As we discussed in the last section about keeping finances separate, there really aren't any *legal* differences between combining or keeping things separate. Being "all in" in this context is purely symbolic.)

For some couples, combining all of your bank accounts is one of the easiest, quickest strategies you can take to use your money to make your marriage stronger.

For others, though, it's one of the *worst* things you can do. Here are a few indications that combining everything—at least right away—is the *wrong* choice for you to make.

Maintaining (some) financial independence is important to one (or both) of you. When you combine all of your bank accounts, there is nowhere to "hide." Every single transaction will be visible to your spouse. There's no hiding anything. There are plenty of circumstances where this level of transparency is a good thing. But like most good things, there can be such a thing as "too much."

Particularly if you're getting married later in life, you've likely had 100% financial autonomy for years. You probably haven't had to answer to anyone about the financial choices you're making since you moved out of your parents' house.

And while it's true that marriage generally changes that, shifting from this environment to having 0% financial autonomy can be a real struggle for couples.

Not to mention, sometimes it's a *good* idea to hide financial transactions from your spouse. Shopping for your spouse's birthday, anniversary, and holiday gifts can be a lot easier when you have a separate checking account!

It's completely okay to want some financial independence in your marriage. As we mentioned in Chapter 6, one of the most common financial differences in a marriage has to do with how much each spouse values being independent versus interconnected financially. If you think this might be true for you or your spouse, I'd—at a minimum—ease into combining all of your accounts. You can always revisit this down the road.

Your spender/saver disparities are high: If you and your spouse are inclined to fight about money in general, it might be a bad idea to combine all of your accounts. But this is *especially* true if most of your fights relate to spending decisions.

Most marriages have one spouse who enjoys saving money more than the other spouse and vice versa. If these types of disagreements are common in your family, combining accounts can be the equivalent of shining a spotlight on these differences—at least until you work on managing these conflicts by using the strategies we learned in Part 2.

Option 3: Yours/Mine/Ours

Back in August of 2017, I had the opportunity to hear Farnoosh Torabi speak at a financial planning conference in Dallas, TX.

Torabi is a personal finance expert and the host of the (fantastic) *So Money* podcast. She is also the author of one of my favorite books on the intersection of money and marriage: *When She Makes More: The Truth About Navigating Love and Life for a New Generation of Women.*

Her presentation at the conference was essentially a summary of *When She Makes More*, and I was hooked. As I've previously mentioned, 2017 was right around the time I was starting to explore the intersection of money and marriage, and her perspective on the topic was a breath of fresh air for an industry that usually downplays or contorts relationship dynamics around money.

I enjoyed her presentation so much that I pulled out my phone and ordered *When She Makes More* while she was speaking. Before her presentation was over, I had placed the order for the book.

The book primarily focuses on relationship dynamics in marriages where the woman is the primary breadwinner. I've learned a lot from Torabi over the years and have incorporated some of her ideas into my financial planning work. But it was her perspective on having some—but not all—bank accounts combined that I found particularly interesting.

The approach that Torabi recommends, and the approach that I recommend as well for many couples, is to have three different types of checking accounts and/or credit cards:

- "Your" bucket: a separate pool of money that your spouse has sole discretion over. This serves as your spouse's personal spending money and "slush fund." Your family budget and goals should dictate how much goes into your spouse's personal bucket, but generally, 10%–20% of their income is a good target.

- "My" bucket: just like the separate pool of money your spouse has, this is *your* personal spending money to do with what you please. Again, 10%–20% of your income should be a good target for how much to put into this fund each month.

- "Our" bucket: the rest of your family's income should go into a joint account to pay for your joint expenses and fund your joint savings goals. Depending on how much you set aside in the "Your" bucket and the "My" bucket, somewhere between 60% and 80% of your combined incomes should be going into the shared account.

The net effect of this is that most of your family's expenses operate out of the joint account, but you are intentionally setting aside personal spending money each month that you have complete control over. The result is that you maintain some degree of financial autonomy while still having the majority of your income working toward your shared financial goals.

OPTION 3: YOURS/MINE/OURS

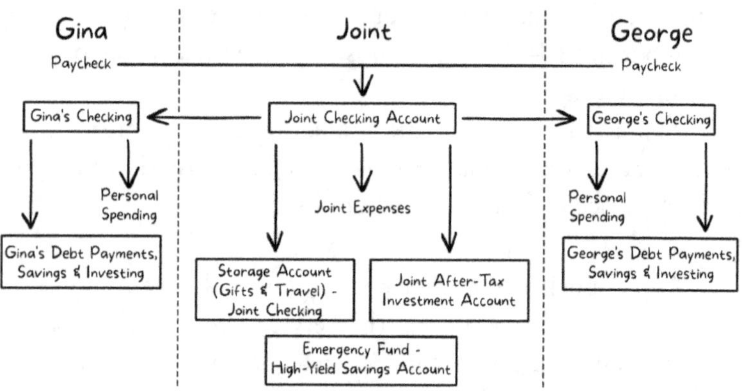

The Yours/Mine/Ours approach works well for many couples for a number of reasons:

It decreases money fights by giving you some "no questions asked" spending money. If most of your family's income is in your joint account to fund your living expenses and your family's financial goals, and you both agree on how much goes into your personal accounts each month, this money can be spent guilt-free. By giving each of you some financial autonomy and a personal spending budget, the number of day-to-day money fights about spending decisions tends to go down—which is a good thing![7]

It makes buying into your budget and joint savings goals easier. Sometimes, people feel threatened when a spouse approaches them about setting aside money for savings goals or getting started on a budget because, even if the spouse doesn't mean it this way, what they

---

7. This is only a good thing if you do the first part—intentionally sit down and agree how much needs to go into the joint accounts to fund your goals, and then agree to how much should go into the personal accounts. If you're just keeping some separate accounts to avoid tough financial discussions—or worse, to hide spending from your spouse—this isn't actually solving the problem; it's making the problem worse.

hear is that they need to cut back their personal spending. By setting a jointly agreed-upon personal spending budget from the outset, it can make the conversation feel less threatening and make it easier for your spouse to get on board.

It makes it easier to buy your spouse gifts. This one is an under-rated reason to have some money outside of your joint accounts! When you only have money in shared joint accounts, it's hard to buy your spouse gifts without them knowing about it. By keeping some money off to the side, you can splurge on your spouse without them knowing!

One important note about this account structure: if you're going to implement the Yours/Mine/Ours approach, automating the transfers between accounts is absolutely critical. You don't want to put yourselves in a position where you need to remember to log into your accounts after every pay period to transfer money into your joint account to cover the joint expenses or vice versa.

Agree to how much should go into the joint and personal accounts from each paycheck, and either set up an automatic transfer to move the money or change your direct deposit at work to automatically split up the money between accounts. The easier it is for you to stick to the plan, the more likely you'll follow through!

That being said, the Yours/Mine/Ours approach isn't right for everyone. If one or more of the following applies to you and your spouse, you may want to consider one of the other approaches recommended in this chapter:

You're using separate accounts as a way to avoid having tough money conversations. If you've successfully worked your way through the exercises in this book up until this point, you're good. You've already proven that you're not afraid to dig into the weeds with your spouse! But if you're looking for separate accounts to be a Band-Aid to fix the problem without doing the other work in this book, funneling money into your separate accounts might make the problem worse.

You want a simple approach to managing money as a family. There's no denying that having one—and only one—joint checking account that all your family's income and spending flow through is the easiest way to go. If you and your spouse highly value simplicity over the other factors we've covered in this section, you should consider combining all of your accounts.

Your saver/spender differences are low. If you don't really fight about money—and have regular productive conversations about money—a Yours/Mine/Ours account structure is likely overkill. Don't try to fix a problem that isn't there. If you're not fighting about money, combining your accounts is a perfectly fine approach to take.

It's really important to you and/or your spouse, for religious or cultural reasons, to be "all-in." To be clear, it is 100% possible to be "all-in" on your marriage and have some separate financial accounts. But, for some people, they don't want to consider keeping *any* money separate for religious or cultural reasons. When your reason for wanting to combine everything is strong enough—or, to put it differently, if your family's mission statement calls for you to combine everything—a Yours/Mine/Ours account structure isn't the optimal choice.

At the end of the day, I almost always recommend that couples either use the Yours/Mine/Ours account structure or combine everything, depending on the factors we've covered in this chapter.

OTHER ACCOUNT
ARCHITECTURE DECISIONS

Of course, combining accounts versus not combining accounts isn't the only decision you and your spouse need to make when mapping out your family's ideal financial account structure. There are several other types of accounts to consider. Here are a few principles you should keep in mind:

Consider adding a sinking fund or "storage" account. Your budget might call for you to spend $7,000 each month, but we all know that you're not literally going to spend $7,000 each month. You have some types of expenses that you spend consistently over the course of a year but not literally every month.

Several types of expenses should be built into your budget that you *won't* be spending every month. Some examples include:

- Travel: If you set a $3,000 travel budget for the year, you might spend the $3,000 in only one or two months out of the year.

- Gifts: If you set a $1,000 annual budget for gifts, you might spend some of that in the months when you have family birthdays or anniversaries and the rest around the holiday season.

- Insurance premiums: Often, life insurance, disability insurance, and auto insurance premiums will be due once a year. If you spend $2,000 per year on these types of insurance premiums, these expenses could hypothetically all happen in one single month of the year.

For each of these items, you need to be careful to set this money aside throughout the course of the year so that you have it when you need it. For these types of planned but infrequent expenses, I often recommend that couples set up a **sinking fund** or **storage account.**

This storage account is usually a second joint checking or savings account that is used to fund these types of irregular expenses. Here's how it works:

- In the above examples (travel, gifts, and insurance premiums), the total annual budget for these three items was $6,000 per year. This averages out to $500 per month.

- You will therefore set up an automatic transfer from your

primary checking account(s) into the storage account for $500 per month so that, over the course of the year, you are intentionally setting aside enough money to cover these expenses.

- When the time comes to pay the insurance premiums, buy gifts, or go on vacation, you'll pay for these items from the storage account. (Depending on the timing, you may need to "front load" the storage account with some money so you don't overdraft while you get the ball rolling!)

- You will then continue to replenish the account with $500 per month.

STORAGE ACCOUNT

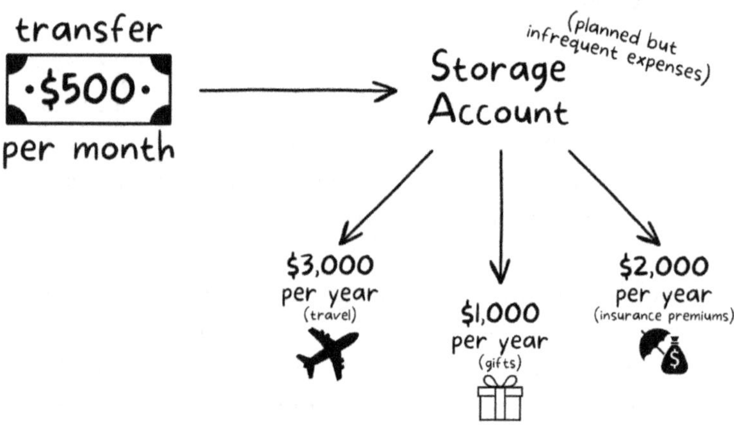

Implementing a storage account is a great way to intentionally set aside money to make it easier for you to fund these types of expenses when they do arise without blowing up your budget.

Your account structure should make it easy to track your progress. In Chapter 10, we discussed your various short- and long-term savings goals, and we identified how much money you wanted to set aside each month to fund these goals. That begs the question: where are you putting this money?

You want to open and/or consolidate financial accounts to be in line with the goals you are setting. There are a few key points to consider while doing this:

- Have (at least) one account per goal. Every goal you set should have a separate pool of money dedicated to working toward that goal. It's okay to have *more than one* account per goal if you want to keep your accounts separate or for retirement (which we'll discuss in a moment), but you should have a separate account for each goal.

- Don't commingle accounts. Along the lines of having one account per goal, you should *not* have an account that is designed to fund more than one goal. When you do this, it makes it very hard to track whether you're on pace to achieve your goals or not because it's not clear how much of the money you have is for each goal. If you're saving for an emergency fund and a new car, you should have two separate buckets of money—one for your emergency fund and one for a new car. It might feel like overkill to have separate savings accounts for separate goals, but it makes it much easier to see your progress over time.

- Have the right type of account for each goal. For things like your emergency fund and short-term savings goals, it's a good idea to use a high-yield savings account and keep the money in cash. For longer-term savings goals, you should utilize investment accounts so you can invest your money to grow over time. And for any goals that have specialty accounts associated with them (e.g., 401(k)s and IRAs for retirement, 529 accounts for college savings, etc.), you should utilize these accounts to take advantage of the tax benefits.

Retirement accounts are always separate. There's no such thing as a "joint" retirement account. Even if you decide to combine your bank accounts, credit cards, and non-retirement investment accounts, your retirement accounts will always need to be legally separate accounts.

You can certainly treat them as joint accounts in spirit and agree to share all of your money in retirement. But while we're talking about combining accounts, it's worth noting that you will always have separate retirement accounts.

At the end of the day, your family's money differences, financial values, and mission statement will dictate the best type of account structure for you.

Ultimately, the most important thing is that your money should be working toward a common goal. As long as the account structure you've chosen—separate, combined, or blended—supports this, you're probably on the right track. If it doesn't, or if you find yourself arguing with your spouse about money, it might be time to make a change.

Regardless, you should take the time to make any needed changes to your account structure before proceeding. I see a lot of couples get stuck at this step of the process. They take the time to figure out the right account structure but drag their feet when it comes to implementing their plan.

So, consider this your call to action. It isn't fun to spend time and energy opening and closing bank accounts, but as you've seen from this chapter, it can be a *lot* easier to accelerate your financial progress—and marital happiness—when you do. So, get to it!

CHAPTER 12

Budgeting

My love/hate relationship with budgeting began on December 22nd, 2011.

I had graduated college six months earlier and was just getting started on my own financially. Overall, I thought I was in pretty good shape. I was lucky that I had a good job and got a small signing bonus. Being the good planner I am, I invested in the stock market with the goal of buying an engagement ring with the funds someday.

But I had some student loan debt to pay off, so I did what everyone always told me to do—make a budget.

I didn't really *want* to, but I knew it was the responsible thing to do. I created an account with one of the most popular online budget-tracking platforms at the time, synced my checking accounts and credit cards to the software, made some educated guesses about what my food, transportation, and entertainment spending might look like, and got ready to start tracking my progress.

And then, the emails started. Specifically, this doozy of an email on December 22nd, 2011:

"You spent $24 at coffee shops this month, and you only budgeted $20. You are a budget failure, and you should probably just give up now."

Okay—I made up the last sentence, but the email is real. That was the day I learned why people hate budgeting.

Who wants to spend the time and effort to be diligent about where your money is going, only to be told that you have no sense of self-discipline by an algorithm because you got an extra coffee that month?

I have long since forgotten anything else that happened in my budget that month, but I remember that email vividly. It left a black mark on my financial planner soul. (Just for fun, I went back and checked my email history as I was writing this chapter. It turns out I had saved $1,602 that month—in December, typically my highest spending month with holiday gifts and travel. But sure, let's get upset about the $4 coffee.)

That's when I realized—there has to be a better way. A way that focuses on the big picture and only goes into the details when you need to. A way to budget that isn't focused on cutting out every last coffee, but one that focuses on the stuff that's most important to you.

Budgeting is important—but it's even more important to approach it the right way.

And as frustrating as I found budgeting for myself in the early stages of my career, at least my budget was relatively straightforward in that I was managing money on my own. Making the shift from budgeting on your own to budgeting with a spouse can be *extremely* difficult to get right.

Because while budgeting is important for everyone, it's *especially* true once you get married. Done incorrectly, managing your money is twice as hard when there are two people involved. But by approaching budgeting the right way, you won't just move forward financially— you'll make your relationship stronger, too.

WHY BUDGETING DOESN'T WORK FOR MOST COUPLES

A lot of the couples I talk to treat "budgeting" like a four-letter word. The reason why so many people despise the idea of budgeting can vary—whether people have had bad experiences budgeting in the past like I did, or they've tried to follow a budget and it just hasn't stuck, or budgets make them feel deprived, or budgets have caused them to fight with their partners, or anything in between—but most people I talk to *hate* the idea of sitting down to do a budget.

And yet, we all know that budgeting is frequently held up as the key to financial success. It doesn't take more than a quick Google search on personal finance and budgets to see the overwhelming evidence that successfully managing a budget is one of the most important factors to succeeding financially.

So, where's the disconnect? If budgeting is as unpleasant as a trip to the dentist, and yet it's as important to your financial health as brushing and flossing are to your oral health, how do we bridge this gap? How do we approach budgeting in a way that you and your spouse will actually stick with in the long run? And ideally, how can we approach your family's budget in a way that will strengthen your relationship rather than be a source of stress on your marriage?

There's a lot of good news on that front. Done correctly, budgeting can be *much* less painful—and much more effective—than you might expect. If, that is, you approach it with the right perspective, goals, and expectations in the first place.

Before building your family's (new) budget, it's worth considering how most couples approach budgeting the wrong way, which prevents their budget from sticking and hinders their growth.

Here are the biggest mistakes I see couples make when it comes to budgeting:

They treat budgeting as the focal point of the journey rather than a tool to use along the way. Too often, when we talk about budgeting, we only focus on the budget itself and the numbers that comprise it. When I ask clients how their budgeting has gone in the past, they tend to start diving into the numbers immediately.

But the point of a budget isn't *just* to hit your numbers. Instead, we budget so we can accomplish our savings goals and live out our mission statements. Without focusing on this dream for the future and how your budget can help you get there, budgeting becomes a dreary, cumbersome exercise. It's no wonder it is such an unpopular activity! But by focusing on your budget as a tool in your pocket to use to help you live your dream life, you will have much better results sticking to your budget in the long run.

They interpret "we need to budget" as "we need to cut our spending." Simply put, the point of a budget is *not* to force you to cut back your spending.

Rather, the *only* goal of a budget is to understand where your money is currently going.

Once again, we turn to the guidance of Carl Richards, who has a few great exercises to help you learn how to approach budgeting as an act of awareness. When you create your first (or your next) budget, the goal is *only* to budget so that you are fully aware of where your money goes each month. Richards takes it a few steps further, encouraging his readers to start budgeting not by setting spending goals across different categories but instead by forcing yourself to pause for three seconds after each purchase you make. "I just spent $30.44 on Amazon shopping for a mirror for my bedroom wall. Isn't that interesting?" If you do this for a month or so, Richards argues, you will notice yourself spending money on things that aren't all that important to you, and you will adjust your spending accordingly.

I recommend you do a little more planning in advance than this method (but if you're really dead set on not planning a monthly budget in advance, Richards's approach would be a great one to try instead!) But what I like about his approach to budgeting is that it tackles the subject with the right perspective.

You should *not* sit down with your spouse and be prescriptive right out of the gate about the need to cut your household spending by 10% this month. Instead, approach the budgeting exercise with the spirit of trying to understand where your money goes each and every month. After all, how could *understanding* possibly be a bad thing, right?

(Of course, you *might* decide to cut some spending at the margins after going through the budgeting process. We will touch on this at the end of the chapter. But the key takeaway, for now, is that even though you *might* cut your spending as a result of your budgeting work, that would only happen as a result of the increased *understanding* you have about where your money goes. It certainly isn't the *point* of the budget!)

They make budgeting too difficult, too complicated, and too granular for them to manage in the long run. Every now and then, I meet a couple who actually *wants* to track their spending at coffee shops on a month-to-month basis. Occasionally, I'll come across a couple who actually *enjoys* tracking granular data and putting together complicated budget progress reports month in and month out.

For most of us, though, this is the wrong approach. There might be circumstances where it's worth digging into the transaction-level data to pinpoint where things are going wrong, but generally, the more time you spend reviewing your bottom-line financial numbers, the better. If you hit your spending and savings targets in the aggregate, there's no need to drive yourselves crazy digging through the weeds.

They view budgeting as restrictive. Raise your hand if you've ever been tempted to touch the plate at a restaurant after your server brings you your food and warns you, "Careful, the plate is very hot!"

It's human nature to want to do something when we are told not to. This means if you approach budgeting in a restrictive way ("I can only spend $20 at coffee shops this month!"), then your immediate gut reaction is likely to be to *want* to spend money at coffee shops.

These types of restrictions usually only last so long before something has to give. And often, what gives is a spending spree that blows up your budget.

Instead, I recommend approaching your budget as a way to spend your money guilt-free. In creating your budget, you and your spouse will agree to how much spending is appropriate for each of you, given your income, fixed expenses, and other goals. By definition, you can spend everything in your budget without worrying or feeling guilty. By following the plan you create for yourselves, you're setting your family up for less financial anxiety by not just protecting your financial goals but actually giving yourselves permission to *enjoy* the money you are spending.

HOW TO BUILD YOUR FAMILY'S BUDGET (WITHOUT FIGHTING ABOUT MONEY)

The short answer is to complete a budget planner for your family.[8] You can access the budget planner that I recommend for Marriage-Centered Financial Plans, along with all of the other resources to help you work through this book, at marriagecenteredmoney.com/resources.

Of course, sitting down and completing a spreadsheet with your partner isn't a magic bullet to having complete clarity and an accurate understanding of where your money is going as a family. In fact, approaching this budgeting conversation haphazardly is one of the easiest ways to start a fight about money.

So, as you put together your estimates for your annual spending across each of the budget categories, I recommend keeping these key themes and tactics in mind as you prepare the budget with your spouse:

Start with your mission statement and goals. If you take one thing from this chapter on budgeting, this should be it.

People fight about budgets and spending when they are only looking at the savings and spending numbers and not considering *why* they are looking to save money in the first place. By anchoring the conversation around what the budget will allow you to accomplish, you're going to get a lot more from the conversation.

You both have already agreed to your family mission statement and your specific financial goals. And your family budget is the map that will help you reach these goals.

Once you've agreed on your mission statement and goals, it usually

---

8. I can feel some of you cringing at the thought of sitting down to budget your spending category by category (and maybe even feeling a bit let down after everything I've said so far in this chapter!). Don't worry—as you'll see in the rest of this chapter, I *don't* recommend tracking your budget at the category level in the long run. Completing a detailed budget planner is a one-time activity!

is *much* easier to agree on the bottom-line budget. By focusing the conversation on how you can achieve the goals and desires you've already articulated, you are empowering yourselves to identify how the budget can help you make these things a reality. This tends to make for a *much* more productive and peaceful process when setting your family budget.

Be mindful of your financial differences and money scripts. The exercises you completed in Part 2 about you and your spouse's different money histories and financial perspectives weren't just to help you forge a deeper connection with your spouse—although I do hope this was a byproduct of those exercises!

On the contrary, one of the key components of a Marriage-Centered Financial Plan is actively taking these principles into account when working on your finances as a family.

So, as you complete your family budget in this chapter, you should pay close attention to the way you and your partner discuss areas you've already uncovered that are likely to lead to differences. You and your spouse's money scripts heavily influence the way you make spending decisions—and in places where your money scripts are opposites, this creates fertile ground for financial arguments.

It's important that the final version of your family budget respects both of your perspectives and strikes the right compromises to make sure each of your individual needs is appropriately addressed in the pursuit of your family mission statement and financial goals.

As you might guess, the most common financial difference that tends to create problems for families when they create their budgets is between the "saver" and the "spender" in the relationship.

In completing your family budget, the "spender" will have to accept the need for some parameters on how much money can be spent as a family. But—and this is important—the spender gets quite a bit of say in what those parameters are! So, if you're the "spender" in your marriage, you need to accept there will be some new guardrails set around how much money can be spent on a monthly basis. (Although, again, the good news is that you get a say in what those guardrails should be!)

On the other hand, the "saver" is also going to need to accept that as a family, their budget might not call for as much money to be saved as they have saved in the past or as much as they would like to save each month. Your family budget is going to give your spouse (and you!) permission to spend up to a certain dollar amount per month, and you need to accept these terms to move forward. Although, again, you *also* get a say in what the overall savings number should be.

The other common financial difference that tends to flare up in these budgeting conversations is the habits of the "hands-on" spouse versus the "hands-off" spouse. The hands-off spouse likely will find the granular nature of going through your budget category by category to be exhausting and unnecessary. (The hands-on spouse, on the other hand, might wish they were doing a *deeper* dive!)

Here's my challenge to the hands-off spouse when it comes to setting your family budget: go through the exercise in as much detail as you can *once* and *only* once. I promise that you aren't going to be asked to dig deep into each and every budget category month in and month out. (See Chapter 15 on the Monthly Money Meeting structure for some reassurance there—if you'd like!)

We need to go deep just this once to get the full lay of the land when it comes to your income and expenses. Once you do this, you will only need to go into the weeds on specific parts of your budget (rather than the whole thing) *if*, and *only* if, something goes wrong.

Most hands-off spouses find the initial process to be cumbersome, and it honestly *is* a little cumbersome. But the good news is that you only need to do it once!

Don't use historical spending estimates (within reason). Whenever I ask couples to create a budget, the first thing that tends to happen is that they pull out historical credit card statements to try to start figuring out what their budget should be. "We usually spend $750 per month at restaurants, so I guess our budget for restaurants should be $750 per month."

The problem with this approach to creating a budget is that it's a *great* way to focus your budget on cutting spending—which we've already agreed is the wrong way for your family to create a budget.

Remember, you've come a *long* way in the way you think about and approach money as a family since you started working through this book. The way you make financial decisions going forward—focusing on your family's mission statement, finding the right balance between your financial differences and money scripts, and prioritizing your family's financial goals—likely looks *very* different than the way you've made financial decisions in the past.

So, use this opportunity as a way to approach your family's financial decisions with a clean slate. You've taken the time to articulate your family's financial priorities going forward—let these priorities dictate your future budget.

That being said, you don't need to take this to the extreme. If you want to go back and look at your family's average water utility bill or double-check your auto insurance premiums using your historical spending, that's totally fine. Historical spending can be a great way to quickly pull together your fixed expenses.

Just understand that there are a lot of areas where you budget will likely look different going forward than it did in the past. Some categories may have less spending than they used to, and others may have *more* spending than before. (It's very common, for example, for couples to increase their charitable giving budget after putting together their family mission statement.)

Don't let your past spending dictate your future—this is your chance for a fresh start!

Don't forget periodic expenses. Raise your hand if you've ever come back from a vacation to a huge credit card bill and you weren't sure how you were going to pay for it.

It happens to everyone at some point or another. We get into a good rhythm of maintaining a monthly budget, and then a huge, one-off expense throws one month completely off the rails.

You should be sure to include periodic expenses (spending that you know is going to happen regularly but not frequently) into your budget for the year and set aside money accordingly, using the storage account strategy you learned in Chapter 11.

By setting aside your annual budget in the categories where you only spend money once or twice a year (such as gifts and travel) in a separate storage account, you'll be sure to have the money available when it's time to be spent.

Include joint and individual expenses in your budget. We've talked about the decision to combine some, all, or none of your money and how to make any of these choices work.

But I *highly* recommend that you have at least some joint *and* individual expenses in your family budget—regardless of which account structure you've chosen.

If you've decided to keep everything separate, you still are going to have *some* amount of joint expenses. Your lives will be easier if you create at least some items in your budget as joint expenses, such as your rent or mortgage payment, your internet bill, and your groceries. You can split them evenly or proportional to your income if you'd like, but to make things easy for yourself when coming up with your family budget, decide on joint expenses together.

On the other hand, even if you've decided to combine all of your bank accounts, you *should* build some personal spending into your budget. Remember, you're trying to set up your budget as a family in a way that will minimize any fighting about money down the road.

And even if you and your spouse really want to pool *everything* financially, the fact remains that you *will* have expenses that are yours and yours alone going forward. (Unless you and your spouse share clothes and haircuts, those two categories might be a good place to start when planning your personal spending.)

So, do yourselves a favor and make sure that your individual personal spending is at the appropriate level in your budget. Rounding down personal spending in your budget is one of the fastest ways I've seen couples start fighting about budgeting one or two months in ("You told me you were only going to spend $50 on yourself last month, but you spent $200!"), so make sure your personal spending estimates are realistically high enough.

REVIEWING YOUR BUDGET

Once you build your budget at the category level, the *only* things that matter are your total spending and savings numbers. In order to build a budget that's accurate, you *need* to set some granular targets for yourself. You can't say, "Our budget says that we are going to spend $6,000 per month and save $2,000 per month" if you don't calculate that $6,000 per month spending number accurately. This necessarily involves breaking your spending down into $1,750 per month on rent, $700 per month on food, and so on.

But once you've calculated each of your spending targets at the category level, the *only* things that matter are the bottom-line total spending and saving numbers. As I alluded to at the beginning of the chapter, I really don't care if you spend $20 or $200 per month at coffee shops. The *only* thing I care about is if you are saving as much money as you agree to each month.

So, once you break down your budget by category, you should look at the total calculated spending and savings your budget projects you to achieve each month. Once you know these numbers, you can double-check a few key things:

Are your total savings and spending targets realistic? If you typically save $1,000 per month and your budget shows you're expecting to save $5,000 per month, that's a sign you may have missed something in completing the budget planner. But if the total spending and saving numbers are in the ballpark of where you'd expect them to be, that's a good sign that you made a good first pass through the budget.

Is the total monthly savings rate sufficient to help you achieve your goals? This is where we need to check the budget planner against the goals you identified in Chapter 10. If you set a goal of saving $500 per month for a new car and $1,500 per month for a down payment on a house, you would want your total monthly savings rate in your budget to be $2,000 per month. If you find the savings amount in your budget isn't sufficient to meet the financial goals you have, then—and only then—would I recommend going through the budget in more detail to find the most efficient places to cut spending (or earn extra income) to make sure you're able to hit your goals.[9] We'll discuss the easiest way to make spending cuts to your budget later in this chapter.

On the other hand, if your savings rate in your budget *is* enough to hit your financial goals, *do not go through your budget with a fine-toothed comb to try to find places to cut your spending.* If you are able to save as much money as you need to in order to realize your family mission statement, you've won the budgeting game. By definition, you can feel free to spend everything else guilt-free since you're doing enough to hit your savings goals as a family!

Once you have a realistic budget that will allow you to hit your savings goals, it's time to stop tinkering with the budget. If you need to save $2,000 per month and can consistently do that even if you spend $200 per month at coffee shops, that's great. Go spend the $200 at coffee shops guilt-free—you're doing everything you need to do financially. There's no point in digging into the weeds if you're saving enough money to accomplish your goals.

CUT YOUR SPENDING CAREFULLY AND INTENTIONALLY

If you do decide that you need to cut spending in order to fully fund your goals, you should find the easiest, most impactful places to cut.

Remember, we aren't actually cutting spending in your budget unless you *need* to in order to hit your financial goal targets. But if you *do* find yourself needing to make spending cuts, you should try to find the easiest and most efficient places in your budget to do so.

---

9. Alternatively, you could utilize some of the other strategies we covered in Chapter 10 relating to how to prioritize your goals in these circumstances.

The mistake I see too many couples making when they try to cut their expenses is that they start cutting from categories that do very little to move the bottom-line spending numbers but cut a lot of joy and pleasure out of their life.

So, before you start cutting your Netflix subscription or $20 per month Starbucks expenses from your budget, take a look at these two things first:

Ask yourselves, "What money are we spending on stuff that isn't really important to us?" If you can come up with clear answers to this question, that's the *first* place I recommend cutting in your budget. I once worked with a couple who, upon going through their budget, realized they were spending over $100 per month on magazines that they barely read and weren't interested in reading—so, they canceled them. This immediately freed up over $100 per month in their budget just by cutting something that wasn't all that important to them. (And yes, I literally mean physical, printed magazines. They still exist, believe it or not!)

Take a look at the three biggest categories in your budget in terms of dollars spent per month and explore ways to trim these first. For most of you, your top three categories are going to be food, transportation, and housing, in no particular order. A 10% reduction in any one of these three areas is going to go a *lot* further than cutting out Spotify Premium. Making changes in these categories sometimes takes a little bit of time (and you definitely *don't* want to cut too deeply in these areas if it will take you further away from your family mission statement!). But it's usually the fastest and most painless way to have results in improving your bottom-line savings target in your budget.

Put differently, don't start cutting your Netflix subscription if you have three cars as a family and only use one of them. Look to make changes in the big categories first—it's likely to do way more to improve your bottom line than removing life's little pleasures from your budget, and it will probably have less of an impact on your day-to-day enjoyment of life as well!

GETTING YOUR
BUDGET RIGHT TAKES TIME

Be patient with yourselves as you go through this process. You're probably going to suck at budgeting for at least three months, and that's okay!

You should treat your family budget seriously—I recommend treating it as a promise to your partner that you are going to try your best to follow—but you also need to give yourselves a bit of grace. It's going to take you a few tries to fine-tune your budget appropriately.

Most couples I work with take a few months to really fine-tune their budget. At first, you'll probably underestimate what you're going to spend in certain categories. (Grocery stores and personal spending are the two budget categories I most commonly see underestimated— for what it's worth. It might not be a bad idea to add 10% to your budget in each of these categories right away if you're in doubt that you may have accidentally underestimated.)

Then, you'll discover that you need to fine-tune your budget slightly from month to month. You might get your budget perfected in October, only to discover you overspent by $200 in December when your heating bill jumped.

It will take you some time to get your budget right—this is *completely* normal. For now, just do your best at estimating your family expenses, and recognize that you're not a failure if you accidentally overspend in a budget category or two.

Commit to your partner you're going to do the best you can to estimate your budget and hit your numbers month after month and be committed to the process of fine-tuning as you need to. The good news is that it's a *lot* less work to make minor tweaks to your budget than to get it set up for the first time!

For now, take some time to get your family budget drafted. We'll talk in depth about how to track your progress and evaluate the efficacy of your budget in Chapter 15.

CHAPTER 13

Debt

Tom and Tina were seemingly a match made in heaven. They met at a friend's wedding shortly after college, and it was love at first sight.

They immediately started dating, and all of their friends thought they were the perfect match. They had the same interests and enjoyed traveling around the world together. So, it was no surprise to anyone who knew them that Tom popped the question to Tina after only dating for about ten months, and they got married shortly after that.

Things were going great for Tina and Tom—at least that's the way it seemed. Behind the scenes, the newlywed couple was dealing with a financial issue that threatened to derail their marriage.

At first, Tom and Tina thought they were relatively in sync financially. They both had similar spending habits, and their goals related to retirement and buying a home were in alignment with each other.

But there was one thing about their financial situations coming into their marriage that was very out of balance—their levels of debt.

Tina considered herself very fortunate to have avoided taking on debt as she went through school and the first few years of her career. But Tom was less "lucky." He had accrued over $120,000 in student loans and an additional $10,000 in credit card debt while he was pursuing a graduate degree. A few years into making the minimum payments on this debt, the balances he owed had actually *increased* due to relatively low required minimum payments and high interest rates.

Deep down, Tom was ashamed about his financial situation, and he felt hopeless about how to get out of debt. So, he took the "easy" approach and tried to avoid thinking about it as much as possible.

Tina saw this apparent indifference in his attitude about debt and was concerned about it. But rather than trying to understand *why* Tom appeared so apathetic about his debt, she took it as an omen that he'd never get his financial act together.

So, she decided to insulate herself financially from Tom until he got his financial house in order. She opted to keep all her money in separate accounts, continuing to save as much as she could. Helping Tom with his debt was a nonstarter—at least until he got his act together.

And so, the cycle continued. Month after month, year after year, Tom's financial situation stagnated while he struggled to make the minimum payments on his debt, while Tina flourished financially.

They were able to buy a house—with Tina supplying 100% of the down payment and covering most of the monthly mortgage payment. Outwardly, they looked like they were living their dream lives in their dream house, but due to the nature of their financial dynamics, Tom felt insecure and ashamed that he wasn't able to contribute to their homeownership goal, and Tina felt resentful that she was carrying so much of the burden.

Eventually, Tina had done such a good job saving for retirement that she was able to retire at the relatively early age of fifty-seven. This was, of course, out of the question for Tom. Even a standard retirement age was unlikely for Tom because he had spent so many of his working years chipping away at his debt. So, Tina spent the best part of her retirement years enjoying her financial freedom by herself. It never even occurred to her to treat her retirement accounts as joint accounts with Tom. After several decades of not trusting him with money, why would anything change now?

———

I'll come clean—the story of Tom and Tina is completely fictional. Still, it wonderfully illustrates the very real challenges your relationship faces when it comes to handling debt.

Debt is an incredibly difficult subject for many couples to learn how to handle in the early stages of their relationship. Because so many of us don't start our marriage with a "blank slate" when it comes to debt, we often have very strong emotional reactions to our partner's debts.

Tom and Tina's story shows just how badly things can go if debt issues are left unresolved. The "easy" answer in the short term is to say that your spouse's debt is their own problem to deal with … but the problem is that their debt *will* have an impact on you, even if it shows up in other areas of your financial life as it did for Tina's home-ownership and retirement goals. And that's only looking at the financial side of the Money/Marriage Scale. I glossed over the impact of debt on Tom and Tina's relationship, but I'm sure you can imagine that it would do serious damage to their marriage in the long term.

Simply put, you need to come up with a plan about how to handle debt together. That doesn't necessarily mean one spouse needs to literally pay off the other's debts (although it can!), but you *do* need to have a joint plan that's coordinated with your spouse on how to handle debt.

When we think about coming together to make a decision with your spouse about how to handle debt in your marriage, there are two different "lenses" we can use—how you'll handle future debt decisions and how to handle the debt you've already accrued. Let's consider each of these lenses, one at a time.

WHAT ROLE WILL DEBT PLAY FOR YOUR FAMILY GOING FORWARD?

I find that starting the conversation around debt management looking forward, rather than looking backward, is the easiest place for couples to start because it's more of a blank slate.

When considering your future goals, is debt a tool you and your spouse are going to use together to make financial progress, or is it something that you're going to avoid at all costs?

Are you and your spouse willing to borrow money if you can find ways to achieve a rate of return with that money greater than the interest rate on the debt? Are there any limits to this?

Or are you never going to take out a loan ever again? Are there any limits to this? (For example, even couples who agree they will try never to borrow money again will often make an exception for mortgages.)

Are you going to use credit cards regularly as a family and pay them off every month, or are you going to cut up your credit cards and never use them again?

There aren't necessarily right or wrong answers to these questions, but it's important that you and your spouse come up with a game plan for how you are going to use debt as a family going forward. Here are a few key items to consider as you begin the discussion:

Consider your mission statement. Like most aspects of your Marriage-Centered Financial Plan, your family mission statement should serve as a guidepost in deciding the role of debt in your family.

What's the easiest way for you and your spouse to realize the vision you created in your family mission statement? Is it to use debt frequently, to use debt in a calculated way, or to avoid debt altogether?

Keeping this forward-thinking lens front and center is the key to having a productive conversation around how your family will use debt. "We want to get in alignment on how we handle debt in the future so that we can _______." (And looking ahead a bit, this sort of approach works really well in figuring out how to handle your existing debts, too: "We want to handle our existing debts/pay off our existing debts so that we can _______." But we will get there soon!)

Debt can either be a tool or a roadblock on the journey to realizing your family's mission statement, as long as you decide how to use it intentionally. Start the conversation focused on your family mission statement, which should help guide you toward the proper role debt should play in your family going forward.

Keep your money scripts and financial differences in mind. Your different money scripts and financial differences have a strong influence on the way you should structure your debt plan as a couple.

Couples with strong Money Status or Money Avoidance money

scripts are much more naturally inclined to use debt—whether it be credit cards, auto loans, or anything in between—to manage their day-to-day finances unless they intentionally choose to do otherwise. In contrast, someone with strong Money Vigilance scripts is likely to want to avoid debt.

If you have a strong Money Status/Avoidance money script and your spouse has a strong Money Vigilance money script (or vice versa), this should serve as a warning sign that you need to sit down and very intentionally agree on how to use debt as a family going forward, since your default ways of handling debt are likely different.

The same can be said for some of the other financial differences we covered in Part 2:

- Security versus freedom: People with strong financial security preferences are going to view debt as a threat to that security, and the more freedom-oriented folks are going to be tempted to use debt as leverage to get higher rates of return on their money.

- Saver versus spender: No surprise here—spenders tend to be more inclined or open to the use of debt than savers.

- Value versus quality: Individuals who prioritize an item's quality are more likely to use debt to finance the purchase of higher quality items and often view restrictions on debt as an inhibitor of pursuing these types of quality purchases.

Depending on your money scripts and your financial differences, changing the way you handle debt may not be an easy thing for you to do. That's completely normal, and you should be patient with your spouse while you make the transition to handling debt intentionally as a family.

How strong are your debt preferences? The final thing to consider has to do with how strongly you feel about debt. I've met countless people over the years who *hate* debt in just about every form, who *never* want to use debt for anything, ever again. For individuals with this strong of a feeling toward debt, using debt strategically is a *really* big ask.

On the flip side, I rarely meet people who *love* to use debt. Many people view debt as a strategic tool, but most people don't actively *enjoy* having debt.

In finding the right balance between you and your spouse's perspectives on debt, you should consider the intensity of your opinions about the way to handle debt in your family going forward. If one of you hates debt and is terrified of it, and the other sees the value in using debt occasionally as a strategic tool but is largely indifferent to debt on an emotional level, it might make sense for the family's position on debt to be to avoid it. You should look for ways to compromise or collaborate where both of you can get something you want out of the deal.

It's okay for you and your spouse to have differing attitudes or preferences around debt, but you need to agree *together* on how your family will use debt going forward. There are many ways that you can come to an agreement:

- Deferring to the spouse that hates debt and agreeing to strictly limit the way you use debt as a family…as long as doing so won't lead to feelings of resentment. (This is a great example of the accommodating conflict resolution style we discussed back in Chapter 7.)

- Agreeing to use some specific forms of debt (e.g., a mortgage, credit cards if you pay them off in full each month, etc.) but avoiding others (car loans, personal loans, etc.).

- Approach each debt decision on a case-by-case basis and utilize debt in places where it makes logical sense for your family.

The important thing, for now, is to pick an approach on how your family will use debt going forward and agree to follow this approach.

Once you and your spouse are in alignment on how to handle debt as a family going forward, it's time to figure out how to handle your current debt.

HANDLING YOUR EXISTING DEBT

I can't say it enough: you *need* to come to an agreement on how to handle your existing debt as a family.

You don't necessarily need to literally treat every single credit card or student loan as both of your equal responsibilities to pay off, but you *do* need to agree to a plan as a couple on what to do about your existing debts. The story of Tom and Tina clearly shows the issues in deferring to the status quo and handling things separately—you need to discuss and agree on how to handle your existing debt together.

But there are a few money and marriage landmines scattered throughout this conversation, depending on whether one of you or both of you have existing debt and how much debt you have.

Rather than prescribing a one-size-fits-all recommendation for how you should approach the conversation about your existing debts, I recommend you use the Money and Marriage Debt Matrix, illustrated below, to guide your conversation.

THE MONEY & MARRIAGE DEBT MATRIX

1	2
You & your spouse both have a lot of debt	Your spouse has a lot of debt, but you don't
3	**4**
You have a lot of debt, but your spouse doesn't	Neither you nor your spouse has debt

As illustrated in the Matrix, there are different challenges and pitfalls you will face in your debt payoff journey depending on your starting point. Your approach, therefore, should look a little different depending on which of these four scenarios apply to you:

1. You and your spouse both have a lot of debt.
2. Your spouse has a lot of debt, but you don't.
3. You have a lot of debt, but your spouse doesn't.
4. Neither you nor your spouse has debt.

Just because your starting place in one of the four quadrants might be different than others, the end destination is the same: creating and implementing a plan to manage your debt as a family.

Depending on which quadrant you are in, you'll want to handle the conversation about your existing debt a little differently and watch out for specific dangers related to each quadrant along the way. Let's address each of the four quadrants—one by one.

Quadrant One: You and Your Spouse Both Have a Lot of Debt

Logistically, this quadrant is often the most difficult to deal with when it comes to paying off the debt itself. If you and your spouse both brought a lot of debt into the marriage, it's going to require hard work on both of your parts to pay it off.

From a marriage standpoint, though, this might be the most straightforward quadrant to handle in terms of coming up with a game plan.

You and your spouse both have debt to pay off. Agree on a game plan and commit to working it *together*. The tactics and strategies I recommend for paying off debt can be found at the end of this chapter. Pick the ones you want to use and get to it!

Of course, this is easier said than done—especially if you and your spouse have a *lot* of debt. It's easy to feel hopeless when you are staring at such a big loan balance. And that feeling of hopelessness often leads to avoidance and inaction, which will only worsen the problem.

Here are a few things to keep in mind to help you abandon the feeling of hopelessness and be empowered to get rid of your debt—together:

Pick one thing to focus on at a time. By focusing on one debt at a time and working as hard as you can to pay it off, you'll give yourself some confidence and momentum along the journey.

Reward yourself along the way. Paying off debt requires an intense level of focus and delayed gratification while you work to clear out the debt. Don't be afraid to set some milestones along the way to give you a reason to celebrate as you work through the plan.

You're in it together. The good news about being in Quadrant One is that you and your spouse are united together in this. You both dug the hole, and now you're digging out in lockstep with each other. Lean into each other and rely on each other for emotional support as you go on this journey.

Remember—this is temporary. The sacrifices you are making now to get rid of your debt aren't going to be sacrifices you need to make forever. Stay true to the vision of your family's future that you painted when crafting your mission statement, and use this as inspiration to buckle down now to get your debt cleared up as fast as possible.

Focus on the Five Principles. You are in a fundamentally different place financially than you were at the beginning of this book. You've taken some steps to get control of your finances as a family and to get on the same page with your money. You have clarity around where your money is today and where you want your money to take you down the road. And you have a game plan for how to make this happen. You should feel *much* more confident about where you're heading financially—even if the bottom line hasn't caught up yet. You *can* do it!

Quadrant Two: Your Spouse Has a Lot of Debt, But You Don't

"How are things going to change about the way you manage money after you get married?" I remember asking Edward and Elizabeth in our final meeting before they tied the knot.

"We will be able to start combining finances and managing money together," Edward replied. "We can consolidate our savings accounts, operate out of the same checking account…" he paused. After a moment, he said, "Maybe Elizabeth can help me finish paying off my student loans so I can start contributing more to our household finances?"

Elizabeth visibly pulled back. "Well… it's *his* debt," she said. "I don't think I should need to pay it."

The story of Tina and Tom at the beginning of the chapter illustrates the issues with this approach. There are a few big problems with taking this attitude:

- It might not be your debt, but it *will* affect your family. You married your spouse "for richer or for poorer"; there is no avoiding the fact that their financial situation will affect you. You might not have been part of the decision to take out their debt before you got married, but it *is* your problem now. Even if you don't pay the debt down directly, it *will* affect your financial future—so it's important to have a family plan for how to handle this debt.

- Elizabeth's response to Edward about his student loans not being her problem drove a wedge in their relationship. By staking this claim, his feelings were hurt, and their marriage suffered.

If you married a spouse who had a heart condition that placed some restrictions on the types of physical activities they could do, you (hopefully) wouldn't respond by saying, "It's not my body, so it's not my problem." If your spouse has a heart condition, you can safely assume that it's going to have some sort of effect on your life—if not today, then down the road.

Your spouse's debt works the same way. It might not *literally* be your debt that's causing the problem, but it *is* going to have an impact on you.

The good news is that debt isn't permanent like a heart condition.

It can be fixed, and the more you work in coordination with each other, the faster it will go away.

So, I encourage you to carefully consider how you want to plan as a family to handle your spouse's debt. Think through the optimal approach for your family—both on the balance sheet and how to handle the debt in a way that doesn't breed resentment on either of your parts down the road.

Even if your spouse made some financial decisions in the past you wouldn't have made yourself, which caused them to incur the debt, pay attention to their behavior and attitudes today. If they have taken responsibility for how they've used debt in the past, agreed to utilize debt going forward in accordance with what you've agreed to as part of this chapter, and are serious about handling their current debt, then it's in your best interest to move forward with them and handle the debt as quickly as possible.

Unfortunately, it's very easy to feel resentment toward your spouse if you worked hard to stay out of debt while your spouse made different decisions prior to your marriage. I encourage you to try not to get stuck in the past. Come up with a forward-looking plan for how to handle this debt as a family and execute it.

And while deciding to combine your incomes and paying off as much of the debt as quickly as possible is one approach you can take here, supporting your spouse in handling their debt can take many forms.

It could involve having them focus on using their income to pay down the debt while you cover most of your living costs or savings goals. It could involve something more specific, like filing your taxes separately (and paying more in taxes as a result) to keep their taxable income low while they are pursuing Public Service (Student) Loan Forgiveness (assuming they qualify, but that's a conversation for another day). There are a variety of ways you can support your spouse through the process—pick one that works for your family.

Quadrant Three: You Have a Lot of Debt, and Your Spouse Doesn't

In some ways, this is the mirror opposite of the last scenario. A lot of the same things still apply about managing resentment and working together despite the differences in starting points. (If you have a lot more debt than your spouse, it's a good idea to have them read the Quadrant Two section before you discuss together.)

There's one other relationship dynamic that I left out of the Quadrant Two discussion, though, that is especially important when considering the perspective of the spouse who has most of the debt: managing guilt.

It's easy to feel guilty if you recognize you have burdened your family with debt based on how you managed money in the past. I had a client who had very strong feelings of guilt about their student loan levels and really wanted to avoid placing any sense of burden on their spouse in terms of how they handled the debt going forward. He resisted even talking about accepting help from his spouse for *years* before he finally realized that the quicker the loans were gone, the better off they would be as a family.

Simply put—if you're ready to get serious about intentionally managing your debt, it's time to set the guilt aside and move forward. What's done is done, and the faster you can move forward, the faster you'll move on as a family.

Easier said than done, of course. But if you have struggled with feeling guilty about your contribution to your family's debt levels, the best thing you can do is to get very serious about doing everything in your power to pay off the debt. If you're serious and focused on getting rid of the debt as fast as possible, and you're giving it your all, it's 100% okay to accept help from your spouse along the way.

Quadrant Four: Neither of You Has Debt

This is the "easy" quadrant, as you'd expect. If you don't have debt now and have decided on the role that debt will play in your family in the future, it's time to move on.

Though, the one trap I'd warn you about if you're in Quadrant Four is complacency. If you're not struggling with debt right now, that's great! Just make sure it stays that way.

Watch out for credit card balances that drift higher over time until all of a sudden, you can't seem to afford the monthly payments.

Watch out for accidentally missing credit card payments or taking out a small auto loan because you can afford it, without stopping to consider what you've agreed regarding the role that debt will play in your family going forward.

CREATE YOUR GAME PLAN, AND FOLLOW IT

Once you've agreed on the role debt will play for your family in the future and how to approach your existing debt, it's time to create a game plan for how to handle your debt.

If your goal is to use debt carefully as a tool to help your family move forward, this plan is fairly straightforward. Set some parameters on how much debt you can afford or are willing to take on ("We are willing to borrow up to $30,000 to finance home renovations so we can sell our home in a year"), and pick the optimal debt vehicles you will use along the way ("We are opening a XYZ Bank credit card to use for most of our purchases because it pays good travel rewards"). If you're looking to pursue some of the specific student loan forgiveness programs that exist under current law, do your research and take the steps needed to make sure you're on track to qualify. And so on.

If your goal is to pay down some or all of your debts quickly, there are a few specific tactics we need to discuss:

A note on savings rate. When creating your budget, you should have identified your monthly savings target. Typically, we think of this as the amount your budget expects you will add to your bank or investment accounts each month.

But when integrating your savings rate with your debt paydown plan, **you should count any money you're paying on your (non-mortgage) debt[10] as part of your savings rate.** It might not feel like

---

10. There are several reasons I recommend treating mortgage debt differently than other forms of debt, many of which will be covered later in this chapter. For now, suffice it to say I recommend categorizing your mortgage payments as "housing expenses" and other debt payments as "savings."

you're saving *any* money if your bank accounts aren't growing and you're paying $1,500 per month on your debt, but you are. Whenever we talk about your savings rate in this book, you should include however much you're paying down on your (non-mortgage) debt as part of this figure.

Why? A few reasons:

- If paying down debt is one of your financial goals, this $1,500 per month is directly going to one of your goals. It's not money you're spending on yourself; it's money you're directing toward your family's financial future. Count it as part of your savings rate.

- The $1,500 you're putting toward your debt is building your net worth by $1,500.[11] Whether you put your money in a savings account or on your debt, your net worth is going up either way. So, it's okay to treat debt payments as part of your savings rate.

Focus on one loan at a time. The easiest way to get out of debt is to focus all of your attention on one loan at a time.

You need to make the minimum required payment on all of your loans, of course, but when it comes down to paying extra, you should focus all of your extra payments on one loan at a time rather than trying to pay off all of your debt at once. Once you pay off the loan you're focusing on, you should then redirect everything you were paying on that loan (i.e., the minimum required payment on the loan you paid off and all of the extra payment) to the next loan on your list.

Which begs the question: which loan should you focus on first? If

---

11. For the math nerds in the room: I'm simplifying this to make it as easy as possible to implement. Technically, the interest that you pay on your debt each month is an *expense*, and any repayment of the loan principal is *saving*. Using this example, if $50 of your $1,500 monthly payment covers the interest portion of the payment, then you are technically only "saving" $1,450 since your net worth only increases by this much. But to make things easy on everyone involved, any amount you pay on your debt = saving. (The interest portion of a mortgage payment, for what it's worth, composes most of the mortgage payment for a *long* time. This is one of the reasons I don't count mortgage payments as "saving."

you're going to pay off one loan at a time, what's the starting point? There are two choices that will work, each one of which has pros and cons:

- Option 1: Focus on paying off the loan with the lowest balance first using the "**Debt Snowball**" approach, then continue to pay off your debts in order from smallest to largest. This is usually the approach I recommend because it's a great way to build your confidence. Since you're starting with the smallest debt first, you'll be able to pay off a few small loans quickly before you tackle the bigger balances. Much like the "Quick Wins" we discussed in Chapter 3, this will boost your confidence and increase your commitment to the process.

- Option 2: Focus on paying off the loan with the highest interest rate first using the "**Debt Avalanche**" approach, then continue to pay off your debts in order from highest interest rate to lowest interest rate. This is the mathematically optimal approach because, by getting rid of your highest interest rate loans earlier in the process, you're allowing more of your payments to go toward repaying the loan principal each month. Particularly if you have a couple of loans or credit cards with much higher interest rates than the rest, this could be a good approach for you to accelerate your progress.

One final note on this: regardless of which approach you take, I would limit your focus to your non-mortgage debt. Unless your mortgage is *very* small, it's going to take a long time to get rid of the mortgage, and you should make sure you are adequately saving for retirement and your other goals before tackling such a big debt. Clean up your non-mortgage debt first, using either the Debt Snowball or Debt Avalanche, then move on to fully fund your other goals. If there's anything extra, you can start chipping away at the mortgage if you'd like.

Set targets for yourselves along the way. This one is important—break up your debt paydown goals into manageable chunks to help you stay focused and motivated.

Your targets should take two forms:

- Your target monthly payment amount. How much are you going to try to pay on your debt each and every month?

- Milestones/deadlines to pay off specific loans. Once you choose your approach (the Debt Snowball or Debt Avalanche), you can list out your debts in order of priority and set goals for when each of them will be paid off based on your target monthly payment and any one-off payments you're expecting to be able to make (for example, money from an annual bonus at work).

Handling debt with your spouse can be incredibly challenging, and it's one of the most important areas of your finances to agree on as a team. But for couples who are able to successfully implement a debt management and paydown plan in the context of their Marriage-Centered Financial Plan, it can be one of the most rewarding parts of the journey—both in terms of the effect on their family's finances and on bringing them closer together as a couple.

CHAPTER 14

Career & Location

love Christmas.

Around the holidays, people throw around the phrase "Christmas season" quite a bit, but I take that phrase quite literally. If you've ever walked around a store right after Labor Day, seen the displays of Christmas decorations "already" up, and said to yourself, "It's *way* too early for this. Who in their right minds possibly wants to look at this stuff so soon?" now you know. I start listening to Christmas music the second my hometown baseball team is done playing baseball for the season—typically in late September.

I celebrate the "Christmas season" with the same duration and the same intensity that many people have when celebrating the season of summer. And as part of this celebration, I always try to watch one or two new Christmas movies each year.

This brings us to my cross-country flight to spend time with my in-laws in December 2021, just as I was putting the finishing touches on the first draft of this book. As the flight took off, I scrolled through the list of available movies to watch on the flight, hoping I might find a Christmas movie I hadn't seen before. After scrolling through the list of available options, I picked a film that often makes the list of "Best Holiday Films of All Time" but one that I knew very little about: the 1944 Judy Garland musical *Meet Me in St. Louis*.

As a "Christmas movie," it was something of a disappointment.

Most of the film isn't about the holiday season (or even set in the winter), with one very notable exception: Judy Garland's fantastic performance of *Have Yourself a Merry Little Christmas*, which was written for the film, in the closing minutes.

You might expect, then, that I was disappointed with *Meet Me in St. Louis*. On the contrary, it was the *perfect* film for me to watch as I was finishing this book. It might not have been the Christmas movie I had hoped it would be, but it was a *great* movie to teach one of the most important lessons in Marriage-Centered Financial Planning.

Let me explain.

The movie focuses on the Smith family, who happily lives in St. Louis. There are several different characters within the family, each with their own subplot—many of which, as you might expect from a classic Americana musical, focus on coming of age and falling in love. But the relevant part of the story for our discussion focuses on the father's character arc.

Mr. Smith is a successful lawyer at a law firm in St. Louis. One day, he comes home and announces that his firm is transferring him to New York City for a promotion. It's a great career opportunity for Mr. Smith and will be a wonderful thing for the greater Smith family from a financial perspective, but it also means that the entire family will need to leave their beloved hometown of St. Louis and move to New York.

While Mr. Smith is very excited about the opportunity, the rest of the family, to put it mildly, is not thrilled with this decision. Much of the rest of the film is spent showing the various family members coming to terms with the move, culminating with Judy Garland's character singing *Have Yourself a Merry Little Christmas* to comfort her younger sister on the eve of the move. (If you've never noticed what a sad song *Have Yourself a Merry Little Christmas* is, you will the next time you hear it!)

Eventually, though, Mr. Smith realizes how unhappy the rest of his family is at the prospect of moving to New York. He turns down the promotion, and the family lives happily ever after in St. Louis.

Now, many aspects about how the Smiths handled the potential move to New York are antiquated, to put it mildly. Not the least of which being that Mr. Smith never discussed the implications of taking the promotion with his wife before deciding the family was going to move to New York. Yikes.

But even if we change some of the details of the plot to bring them into the 21ˢᵗ century, it's worth considering the decision the Smith family faced.

Was Mr. Smith wrong to even consider moving the family to New York? Was it even worth discussing the promotion, knowing that his family had its roots deeply planted in St. Louis? He was certainly wrong in the *way* he handled the decision, but was it wrong even to *consider* the promotion in the first place?

If you were presented with your dream job, but it would require relocating your family halfway across the country, would this be something completely out of bounds or something that would be worth seriously discussing?

The answer, of course, depends entirely on your family dynamics. If your family is as deeply rooted in your location as the Smiths were in St. Louis, you might not consider moving for a job, no matter how good the opportunity. On the other hand, if your family enjoys the adventure of discovering a new place and making it home, you might jump at the opportunity presented to Mr. Smith in the movie (in a much healthier way than he did!).

In the early stages of my Marriage-Centered Financial Planning process, I used to address career and location decisions separately. But, as *Meet Me in St. Louis* demonstrates so wonderfully, these factors in your family's financial plan are both critically important to your family's happiness and are often linked together.

WHY CAREER AND LOCATION DECISIONS CAN BE SO DIFFICULT

Many couples feel completely settled with where they live and are on good, stable career tracks that work well for them and their families. But for the couples who either aren't on the same page about these items or are facing tough decisions related to their career or location, these questions can be some of the most difficult to answer in your entire Marriage-Centered Financial Plan.

What makes these decisions so difficult for couples to handle when they come up?

In most cases, they are constrained by one another. You either need to choose a job that's local to the place where you live, or you need to be willing to uproot your family and move for a job in a different area. Granted, with the rise of remote work in the past decade, this challenge is a little less severe than it used to be, but for many industries and occupations, you need to live in the area where you work.

Most couples aren't starting with a blank slate when it comes to career *or* location. Unless you get married right out of high school, you likely already made some big career decisions before your spouse came along. So, your starting point needs to be within the bounds of the decisions you and your spouse have already made regarding your careers. And for most couples, some preexisting conditions favor certain locations to plant your roots as a family. Whether they be places you're already settled down in or places around your extended family, most couples passively decide where to live—at least at first.

Now, the rest of your spouse's financial slate isn't necessarily clean when you get married. As we discussed in Chapter 13, they may have a lot of debt (or, on the flip side, a lot of financial assets) coming into the marriage. But questions related to career and income tend to be "stickier"—it's harder to make significant changes with these items unless you really focus intentionally on them. So, as you start to shift from making career and location decisions by yourself to making them with your spouse, you need to be especially careful to be intentional with how you approach these decisions as a family.

Changes in either of these areas take time. You can decide to implement a budget or start paying down your debt in the next thirty minutes if you really put your mind to it, but you're (hopefully) not going to quit your job or put your home on the market in that amount of time without having the next steps in place. You *can* make changes to either your career or your location, but it takes some time for you to really start feeling the effects of these changes.

HOW TO MAKE CAREER AND INCOME DECISIONS AS A FAMILY

The nature of these decisions often varies significantly from one couple to the next. You should review the questions regarding your career and location against the rest of your Marriage-Centered Financial Plan, communicate with your spouse about the decisions while keeping your money scripts and financial differences in mind, and commit to the process of working together to make these decisions.

Since there can be such variability from couple to couple around the changes that come up in the career and income pillars of the plan, this chapter is going to focus more on the high-level strategy for what to focus on as a family than the specific tactics to use. Here are a few key areas to keep in mind:

Review your mission statement and goals for any changes that *should* happen. One of the most surprising things I've noticed over the years is that many couples make some sort of big career or location change upon going through the Marriage-Centered Financial Planning process.

One of the most common conclusions I see people arrive at upon completing the mission statement exercises mentioned in Chapter 9 is that they *need* to make some changes to career, work/life balance, income, or location as a family.

These changes can take many forms:

- Changing careers to have more of an impact or to pursue work that's more in line with your beliefs.

- Changing jobs to leave a toxic work environment.

- Working fewer hours or teleworking to maintain better work/life balance.

- Leaving the workforce entirely to stay at home with your kids.

- Fulfilling a dream to start a business.

- Moving to your dream location.

- Moving to be closer to your extended family.

- Moving to be further away from your extended family.

- Moving for a sense of "place" (for example, if you've always lived in the middle of the city but have dreamed of living out in the country).

If your mission statement and goals necessitate a change in work or location, now's the time to start making plans for how to make this change a reality. That doesn't mean the changes will be easy to make, but if your first reaction upon going through the mission statement exercises was that a change needs to be made in these areas, now's the time to get the ball rolling.

Review your mission statement and goals against any changes you think *might* happen. The above section discussed changes you identified as a result of going through the mission statement development process that you *should* make for the sake of your family. Many (but not all) couples identify at least one big shift that should occur to fully realize their mission statement when going through this process.

But the interaction between the mission statement and your career, income, and living decisions doesn't end there.

Over time, you or your spouse will be faced with different challenges or opportunities you will need to consider in the context of your Marriage-Centered Financial Plan.

If your spouse is offered their dream job—the opportunity of a lifetime—but it's located on the opposite coast from where your family is living now … is that something that would be the adventure of a lifetime for your family? Or is it a complete nonstarter because you've planted your family's roots where you are living now?

Or, if you were to get a job offer that looks like a fantastic opportunity on paper and would come with a substantial pay increase, but it requires you to travel thirty weeks of the year or work seventy hours per week … is this something you would consider, or would the travel and workload be a deal-breaker?

These sorts of decisions don't come up every year or even every decade … but they *do* come up from time to time. And when they do, so many factors are at play that it can be really hard to make the right decision.

Luckily, you've already developed the tool that can make these types of hard choices much easier: your family's mission statement.

Done correctly, your family's mission statement will help guide you through these tough choices and help you illuminate the right decision for you and your family.

The problem that couples often face is that they try to make these decisions in a vacuum, which can quickly devolve into fighting. Even worse, it can lead you to make your decision based on the wrong criteria, creating a new set of problems that can take years to fix.

By using your family's mission statement as objective criteria to evaluate future career and location decisions, you can get the confidence you need that the decisions you are making are the right ones. These sorts of choices are never easy, but with the help of your mission statement, the choice can be clear.

CHAPTER 15

Monthly Money Meeting

Kelly and Ken were doing fine, financially speaking. And it was wrecking their marriage.

On paper, things looked good for Ken and Kelly. They had decided to combine all of their accounts when they got married a year and a half before I first met them. And it worked pretty well for them, at least for a while.

They both had good incomes and were able to save a decent amount of the money they made each month. This wasn't a couple who was living paycheck to paycheck; they had some positive financial momentum and were making good progress.

Like any couple, Ken and Kelly had their financial differences. Kelly was the "saver" in their marriage. When given the choice, she would rather add $100 to the family nest egg than spend the $100 on something for their family. Ken, meanwhile, wasn't an *over-spender* but given the choice, he preferred to spend money rather than save it.

Kelly was also much more hands-on with the family finances than Ken. She was very interested in personal finance, and he was fairly indifferent to it. So, Kelly was the one in their family who monitored their accounts, paid the bills, made the transfers, and so on.

It's not inherently a bad thing for one person to take charge of most of the family's financial responsibilities. The problem, though, was that they weren't communicating about their money.

Kelly was constantly in execution mode, focused on making the day-to-day financial decisions for the family, and Ken was happy to abdicate his role in the decision-making to her. He knew, after all, that personal finance was more interesting to Kelly than it was to him, and he knew they were making good progress.

Because they were in good financial shape, Kelly was perfectly happy to continue executing their plan, and Ken was happy to let her.

Until, that is, the day that Kelly was reviewing their transactions and saw an expense that Ken had charged earlier in the week. "Did you really need to spend this much on that?" she asked him in frustration.

As is often the case when a "saver" confronts a "spender" about their spending decisions, Ken responded defensively. "I don't see what the big deal is. We save a lot of money. What does it matter?"

As you might expect, the conversation escalated from there.

I met Kelly and Ken when they came to me with questions about an unrelated issue. But as the story above suggests, it became immediately clear that the way that Ken and Kelly communicated about money was putting a strain on their relationship. Or perhaps more to the point, the problem was the way they *weren't* communicating about money until something went wrong, at which point Kelly would criticize Ken, and Ken would get defensive.

The problem Ken and Kelly had *wasn't* that they had different money habits. While the "saver"/"hands-on" combination can be a particularly challenging one to navigate, that isn't inherently the problem Ken and Kelly were having. Both the spending/saving differences and the hands-on/hands-off differences, as we've already discussed, are *completely* normal.

Ken and Kelly simply needed a healthier way of communicating about their finances, and they found it by implementing a simple and effective strategy that I call the *Monthly Money Meeting*.

I've seen couples try to communicate about money in a lot of different ways over the years. And the more I've seen these issues arise, the more I think that a simple, straightforward, monthly check-in on your household finances is the best way to systematize communication about money and financial progress in your marriage.

Even better, this process is incredibly efficient. Done right, the Monthly Money Meeting should only take you about twenty minutes per month. By taking just twenty minutes per month, you can completely revolutionize the way you and your spouse communicate about money together.

STRUCTURING A MONTHLY MONEY MEETING

Part of the reason the Monthly Money Meeting works so well is that it happens frequently enough that you're both aware of the state of your finances but not so frequently that it becomes overwhelming.

The other reason it is so effective is because the Monthly Money Meeting is very structured. You're not just setting aside twenty minutes per month to talk about whatever comes to mind when it comes to your finances. Rather, I recommend that your Monthly Money Meeting follow a four-part process (with some pre-work to complete ahead of time):

0. Prework
1. Celebrate
2. Review
3. Clarify
4. Take Action

Each of the four main steps should take about five minutes to complete, leaving you with a twenty-minute Monthly Money Meeting in total. It might take you a few months to get used to the structure and be able to actually complete everything in twenty minutes, but stick with it, and you'll see progress.

By staying focused on covering the right things in your Monthly Money Meeting, you can efficiently improve the way you communicate about money in your marriage.

20-MINUTE MONTHLY MONEY MEETING AGENDA

Here's how to approach each step:

Pre-Work

It's important to have an organized game plan going into your Monthly Money Meeting to make the best use of your time and to be able to quickly identify what's going well (and what needs improvement). Therefore, I recommend that either you or your spouse take a few minutes ahead of the meeting to get organized.

There are three primary tasks to complete before going into your first Monthly Money Meeting.

First, you and your spouse should set a time to have your Monthly Money Meeting each month. These conversations don't just happen naturally; you need to be proactive about putting them in your calendar. Usually, I find that setting a recurring meeting time on the first day or two of each month in the evenings (after the kids go to bed—if you have them) works best. By scheduling at a time of day (in the evenings) when you typically do not have many commitments, you'll be more likely to follow through on your Monthly Money Meeting schedule on a consistent basis. And by scheduling the meeting in the first few days of the month, you'll be in a great position to review what happened during the prior month before too much time goes by, as well as be able to set clear and achievable goals for the next month before it's "too late" to make financial progress for the new month.

The second thing to do before the meeting begins is to gather your financial data from the previous month so you can review your progress over the past thirty days with your spouse during the meeting. If you use a budgeting app or account aggregator, it should be easy to pull together all the information on where your money went for the month. Otherwise, you'll want to gather your bank and credit card statements for the month so you can review your income and expenses in full for the prior month.

Finally, I recommend bringing a pen and a piece of blank paper to the meeting. Ideally, you'll have a notebook that you use for all your Monthly Money Meetings so you will stay organized and be able to see your progress over time. You certainly *can* use a digital note-taking app, but I find there is something about using a literal piece of paper and pen that helps the information stick better over time.

One other note on the pre-work: this is the only piece of the Monthly Money Meeting that should be completed by only you or your spouse. Typically, the more hands-on member of the family takes the lead in getting all of the financial data organized ahead of the meeting. That is *completely* okay, and it's even encouraged—it can be easier to have everything ready to go if one person is solely responsible for getting everything together. You can also consider alternating who is in charge of the pre-work from month to month if both of you would like to be involved. Experiment over time and find what works best for you as a family.

Part 1: Celebrate

One of the biggest success stories I've seen in the past five years involved a couple—let's call them Henry and Hannah—paying off $250,000 of student loan debt in eighteen months.

This type of herculean effort involves dedicated focus, sacrifices, and, yes, a little luck. Hannah and Henry both had great jobs that paid a lot of money, and they were willing to sacrifice a lot of aspects of their standard of living to help them achieve their goal of finally getting out of debt. These things, combined with a few timely bonuses, finally put them in a position to make a final $30,000 lump sum payment to get rid of the loans in August of 2020. I got a jubilant email from Hannah at the end of August, telling me they finally had paid off the loans.

Two weeks later, I had my next scheduled review meeting with Hannah and Henry. I couldn't wait to get on the call to hear how excited they were to finally be out of debt.

"So … how's it going?" I said with a huge smile on my face when they joined the meeting.

But the smile wasn't returned. "We're worried about a few things," Hannah immediately replied before citing a few tax questions they wanted to address.

I paused for a moment. "We will absolutely, 100% address each of those questions," I said. "But not before we take a moment to celebrate the fact that you just finished paying off a quarter-million dollars of student loan debt. That is *incredible*! Before we dive into the next concern, we need to take a moment to celebrate that huge success."

And so, we did. We took a few moments to reflect on their journey and celebrate how far they had come. And by the time we were done, we addressed their tax concerns … but they also realized the tax fears they had were relatively minor challenges compared to what they had just overcome.

Too often, when it comes to personal finance, we focus disproportionately on what's going wrong. Whenever I ask couples what's on their mind when it comes to finances, it's *always* something bad. Even after we achieve financial goals or are making progress on big goals we have in front of us, we typically focus on the next challenge we see down the road.

This can create real problems for couples. By focusing solely on the challenges you're facing rather than what's going *right*, you are by definition setting yourselves up to only communicate about the challenging parts of your financial picture, which is inevitably going to increase the amount of time you spend stressed and fighting about money.

So, I recommend you take a few minutes at the beginning of your Monthly Money Meeting to celebrate what's going well. For your first Monthly Money Meeting, take five minutes and acknowledge/appreciate what you're doing right as a family when it comes to money in general. For subsequent meetings, you should focus on what you've accomplished over the past thirty days since your last meeting.

No accomplishment is too small. Take a few minutes to celebrate what's going well! And don't be afraid to write a bullet-point list of the items that come up in this part of the conversation at the top of your piece of paper.

To be clear: this is *not* one of those "power of positive thinking," "fake it 'till you make it" type of exercises. There is *nothing* that puts me in a worse mood than pretending things are in good shape when they clearly aren't. You should *not* be lying to yourselves during this exercise.

But I'm also willing to bet if you actually pause for five minutes and think about what you're doing right financially, you'll be surprised at how many things come up that you really *are* doing a good job with. So, take a few minutes to celebrate your wins together.

Part 2: Review

Part of a good Monthly Money Meeting involves reviewing your progress over the past month. After you're done celebrating your wins, it's time to take a few minutes to review how you did the previous month.

There is one—and only one—metric you should focus on in this context: how much you saved last month. That's *it*.

No digging into the individual transactions yet. No judgment on how big or how small the savings number was. Just pull together the information, confirm how much you saved last month,[12] and write it down on your piece of paper.

If this is your *first* Monthly Money Meeting, that's all you need to do for now. You now have your baseline monthly savings rate. That's good enough—no going through the individual transactions, no shame, no blame. You are ready to move on to Part 3.

For subsequent Monthly Money Meetings, you should compare the amount you saved to the target you set for yourselves during your last Monthly Money Meeting (see Part 3 below).

Did you save as much as you intended? Did you save *more*? Or did you miss your target?

Here's the fun part: if you hit or exceeded your savings target for the month, you should move on to Part 3. If you're saving as much as you need to save, there is absolutely no point in reviewing your spending line item by line item. Unless you're doing a quick review to make sure there weren't any fraudulent charges (which isn't a bad idea), you and your spouse should *not* dissect who spent money on what. You've hit your savings targets that you agreed to as a team. What you do with the rest of the money *does not matter.*

The only time you should be digging through your historical transactions is if you spent more than you agreed to during your last Monthly Money Meeting. If you didn't hit your savings targets, I recommend taking a few minutes to determine the cause.

Did you have a one-off, unexpected expense this month that threw your numbers off? If so, that's okay (as long as it doesn't keep happening month after month). These things happen.

Or did one or both of you *actually* overspend? There should be no shame and no blame if you did, but it's important to acknowledge if this happened during the "review" phase so you can adapt for next month.

Again, try to limit the amount of "look-back" time you spend reviewing your last month's information to about five minutes. Don't get too bogged down in this discussion. The goals for the review phase

---

12. Remember: debt payments count as saving, so be sure to include them here!

of the meeting are to get clarity around where your money went last month, confirming whether or not you hit your savings target (starting in your second Monthly Money Meeting), and, only if you *didn't* hit your target, pausing to review what went wrong.

Part 3: Clarify

Once you're done looking backward at the month that's passed, it's time to look forward to the month ahead. Where do you want your money to go this month?

In coming up with this answer, there are a few things I recommend you think about and write down on your piece of paper.

First, I recommend taking a moment to remember *why* you want to save money and recommit to this purpose. The goal of saving money isn't to accumulate the biggest bank account possible. You're saving money to do things in the future that you can't do today. Whether it's to buy a new house, provide for your kids, save for retirement, or anything in between, you're far more likely to hit your savings goals if you focus on *why* you're saving money in the first place.

Take a moment, discuss with your spouse, and recommit to *why* you're looking to save money together. Write this down on the page as well.

As you have subsequent Monthly Money Meetings, your reasons *why* you're saving won't change much from month to month. But you should still take a moment each month to review and recommit to the *why* behind your savings plan.

From there, it's time to agree with your spouse on how much you're going to save this month. Once again, your monthly savings rate is the *only* number you should track on a monthly basis. In focusing on this one metric, you will be focusing on the number one key to making financial progress that is in your control.

To set your monthly savings target, you should start with how much you saved last month. Even if you're not satisfied with how much you saved last month, use your previous month's savings rate as a starting point for the discussion. The *most important thing* in setting your savings target for this month is to make sure that it's actually attainable. I'd rather have you set a savings target of $1,000 this month and hit that savings target than have you set a savings target of $5,000 only to find out the target wasn't realistic.

You should then make a few different adjustments to this number to come up with your savings target for the month ahead.

We all know that some months are different from others. Maybe you had an unexpected car repair last month that set you back $750. Unless you're expecting another $750 repair bill this month, you should adjust your savings target from what happened last month based on what you expect to happen this month. In that scenario, you'd take the savings target you calculated by looking at how much you saved last month and add $750 to it. Since the $750 was spent last month but (probably) won't be spent again this month, you can add the $750 to your expected savings target for the current month.

Of course, this works both ways. Think through what expenses you know you're going to have this month that you *didn't* have last month, and make sure to adjust your savings target accordingly. For example, I typically pay my auto insurance bill every six months. I make sure to set aside money each month to cover the bill when it comes due. But if I know I'm going to owe $500 for my car insurance next month and I know we're going to track the total monthly expenses to see how much got added to our bank accounts, I'll need to reduce my monthly savings target by $500 for next month. It's always better to identify these uneven expenses in advance to prepare ahead of time to make sure you're setting the right targets for yourselves. (Setting up the storage accounts we discussed in Chapter 11 can be a big help with this!)

There's one other adjustment you might need to make to your monthly savings target. If you made changes to your budget in Chapter 12, you will want to adjust your savings target accordingly. For example, if you reduced the spending in your budget by $250, you should add $250 to your monthly savings target.

This is a good point in the process to double-check your savings target for the month against the anticipated monthly savings present in the budget you set in Chapter 12. Generally, these numbers should tie together!

If they don't, and the discrepancy isn't caused by one of the one-off expenses that are unique to the month ahead, this is a sign that either your budget is missing something important or that your savings target for the month isn't realistic. Do your best to review each to determine the root cause of the discrepancy, but don't let yourselves get stuck. It usually takes couples about three months to get into this routine. You can always revisit this at the beginning of next month and use the data you collect in the interim to determine whether your budget or the savings target is off.

At the end of the day, the most important piece is to agree on your savings target for the month—together. You both should leave the Monthly Money Meeting knowing what your savings goal is for the month, agreeing that the goal is feasible, and committing you'll do your best to hit the target over the next thirty days.

Over the years, I've noticed that the couples who consistently have the most success hitting their monthly savings targets treat this process of setting their monthly goal very seriously. This isn't just an exercise where you're going through the motions to check it off your monthly to-do list; you should treat this as a serious commitment you are making to each other.

As a sign of this commitment, I recommend you write down your savings target for the month at the bottom of your piece of paper. And I wouldn't stop there—the couples who have the most success implementing this routine literally *sign* and *date* the piece of paper right below the monthly savings target.

Physically signing the document helps cement the promise you are making to each other.

Does this mean you're breaking your vows to one another if you mess up during the month and fall short of your target? Of course not. Does this mean your marriage isn't going to be successful—financially or otherwise—if something comes up over the course of the month and you aren't able to save as much as you promised to one another? Absolutely not.

All you are promising is to work in good faith to do what you need to do in order to hit the savings target. You're promising to commit to the process and do your best to hit your goals. Things can and will happen—that's normal, and it's a part of the process. Just stay committed to working together, month in and month out, and you might be surprised at how much progress you will make.

Part 4: Momentum

Before wrapping up your Monthly Money Meeting, you should take *one* step together to help make your goal a reality.

Making financial progress in your marriage is all about momentum. You've accomplished a *lot* in the first fifteen minutes of your meeting. You've celebrated your successes, reviewed the previous month's information, and set your goals for this month. Now, it's time to give yourself some momentum for the month ahead.

Look at the monthly savings target you wrote down on your piece of paper. What's *one thing* you and your spouse could do *right now* to help you hit this goal?

It doesn't need to be a huge step, nor should it be something that takes a lot of time. In the next few minutes, what's *one thing* you could do to help make your goal for the month ahead a reality?

For some of you, this will involve paying off your credit cards from last month, so you're starting the month with a clean slate. (It's hard to meet your savings targets when you're still paying for last month's stuff!) It could also involve adjusting some recurring expenses, scheduling automatic transfers into your savings accounts, or setting up some time on your calendar to monitor your progress in the month ahead.

By taking an immediate step to help make your goal for the month a reality, you'll dramatically increase your chances of hitting your target. Take that first step toward hitting your goal before you wrap up your Monthly Money Meeting.

Many couples who go through the Marriage-Centered Financial Planning process cite the Monthly Money Meeting as the most impactful part of the process in terms of its ability to drive long-term financial and marital success.

The reason why this process is so effective for couples who take the time to implement it isn't just because it's an efficient and structured process, although that's certainly part of it!

Rather, it has to do with the Five Principles of Marriage-Centered Financial Planning we covered back in Chapter 2.

Each chapter in this book was designed to improve you and your spouse's standing in one or two of these principles. The Monthly Money Meeting is the rare part of the process that helps you across all *five*.

Confidence: The two fastest ways to build your family's financial confidence are to take time to reinforce what's going right (and not just where you're struggling) and having a plan to take control of your finances. The Monthly Money Meeting does both.

Coordination: The structure of the Monthly Money Meeting is designed to get you and your spouse working together financially by deciding how to make forward financial progress in a way that gives each of you a vote in your financial decisions.

Communication: Having a consistent, established time to talk about your finances while focusing on what matters most and staying out of the weeds as much as possible greatly reduces the likelihood of fighting about money throughout the month.

Clarity: The Monthly Money Meeting is structured around getting crystal clear on where your money went last month and where you as a family want your money to go in the month ahead. It's hard to get more clarity than that!

Commitment: By limiting these conversations to about twenty minutes per month, it's much easier to stick to these routines over time.

Best of all, you'll be taking action to help follow through on your financial goals during the last five minutes of the meeting.

I encourage you to work with your spouse to determine the right day of the week and time of day to schedule your Monthly Money Meeting. Taking this one small step each month will pay dividends to your financial bottom line and to your relationship.

CHAPTER 16

Financial Security & Financial Freedom

One of the most common types of financial differences between spouses involves one spouse that prioritizes financial security and the other that prioritizes financial freedom.

Here's what I said on the subject when we covered this difference back in Chapter 6:

> Within marriages, it's common for one spouse to be financially motivated by the desire to keep the family safe and secure financially. To this spouse, things like avoiding debt, having a healthy emergency fund, and having adequate levels of insurance coverage are *really* important.
>
> On the flip side, the spouse more motivated by financial freedom is primarily interested in seeing their money growing and working for them. To this spouse, debt, for example, is a tool to use to help you build wealth rather than something that should be avoided entirely.
>
> A good Marriage-Centered Financial Plan will give you *both* financial security and financial freedom ... The key, as we will discuss, is working on building your financial security and financial freedom by following the right

sequence of steps, in the right order, and appropriately prioritizing these items as a family.

Financial planners and money experts often talk as though *keeping your money safe* and *letting your money grow to achieve financial freedom*[13] are two opposites. And while it's undeniably true that you need to take investing risk to grow your assets to the point where you can retire, I think this dichotomy misses the mark a bit.

Instead, I believe financial security and financial freedom need to work *together*. You can't achieve financial freedom without having a solid, secure financial foundation for your family. Attempting to do so might look like you're building something spectacular, but without a secure financial foundation, all you'd be building is a house of cards, poised to tumble the first time something goes wrong.

On the flip side, focusing on keeping your money secure without planning for your long-term financial freedom might feel like a safe move to make. But in treating your long-term money this way, you're overlooking the most significant financial risk you are likely to face in your lifetime: inflation.

A gallon of gas that costs \$4–\$5 today only cost \$0.29 back in 1955.[14] You need to be taking steps to make sure you're giving your long-term investments the best possible chance at keeping pace with inflation, or else your money in the future will be worth less than it is today.

You need to focus on *both*—being financially secure in the short term *and* being financially free in the long term. It isn't possible to achieve one without the other. Build a solid financial foundation first, and then build the tower upward.

You've come a *long* way as you've worked through the content in

---

13. Ask ten different people to define "financial freedom" and you're likely to get ten different answers. For the purposes of this book, I define "financial freedom" as being able to pay your living expenses without needing to work. "Financial freedom" and "retirement," then, can be used interchangeably.

14. I wrote the draft of this chapter in early 2021. The initial draft quoted the price of gas today as "\$3-\$4." During my final revisions in mid-2022, I updated the draft to "\$4-\$5." I mention this only because it perfectly underscores the point I am trying to make!

FINANCIAL SECURITY & FINANCIAL FREEDOM

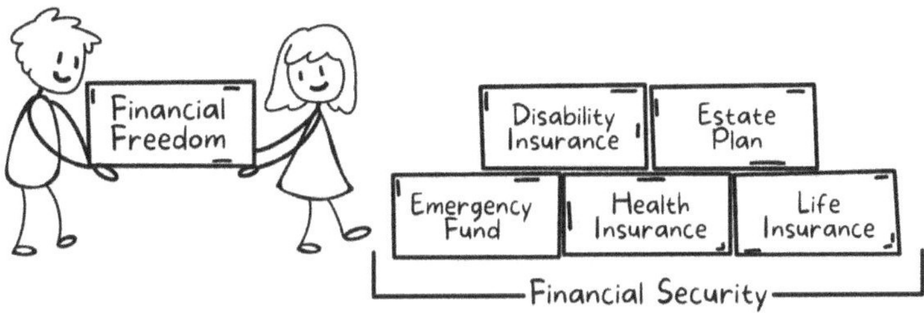

Part 3 of this book. You've developed a mission statement to guide your family's decision-making, and you've set some concrete financial goals to help make this mission statement a reality. You got into alignment with your spouse around your family's budget, debt, and career/location decisions. And you've started an efficient process to track your family's financial progress in the form of a Monthly Money Meeting.

There's only one question left to be answered, and it's a big one. What do you *do* with the money you're saving each month? The answer, as you might suspect from the way I've set up this chapter, is to allocate your savings in a way that bolsters both your family's financial security and financial freedom.

In the first year or two of your Marriage-Centered Financial Plan, you will likely spend most (but not all) of your time focusing on firming up your family's financial security. Once you have built a very secure financial foundation for your family, then your attention will shift to focusing on maximizing your long-term financial freedom.

And so, before we bring this book to a conclusion, I wanted to quickly summarize several of the considerations you should bear in mind when building your Marriage-Centered Financial Plan. Think of this chapter (along with the budgeting and debt chapters) as the stuff that typically would be included in a personal finance book. I've intentionally focused the majority of this book on the "marriage" side of the Money/Marriage Scale, but I wanted to spend a bit of time getting you thinking about the financial components of the plan.

First, we will run through the financial security elements you should consider including in your plan, and then we'll wrap up with a discussion of the financial freedom elements.

Please take this list of ideas as just that—suggestions. Each Marriage-Centered Financial Plan is unique, so I am intentionally focusing on principles, strategies, and guidelines rather than specific tactics for each of these items. (Remember, don't take the prescription until you've been thoroughly diagnosed!)

FINANCIAL SECURITY COMPONENTS OF A MARRIAGE-CENTERED FINANCIAL PLAN

Emergency Fund

Before allocating money toward any of your other goals, I recommend setting aside an emergency fund with enough money to cover three to six months of expenses.

If your household has two incomes, or both you and your spouse are aligned on the "financial freedom" side of the security versus freedom financial difference, three months of expenses should be sufficient. If you're more conservative when it comes to financial risk or are a single-income household, you should have closer to six months saved up.

This emergency fund should typically be a savings account that is separate from the rest of your money that you could access very quickly if needed. Remember, one account for each goal, and your emergency fund should be treated as a separate goal and shouldn't be commingled with anything else. Unless you and your spouse are *very* opposed to combining any money at all for any reason, I typically recommend that your emergency fund be a joint account. (If your spouse were facing a financial emergency and you'd be willing to help them out financially, it's safe to make this a joint account.)

If you can utilize a high-yield savings account to get a slightly higher interest rate on your emergency fund, that's great. If not, no worries. The point of your emergency fund isn't to make a lot of money on interest—it's to keep the rest of your money safe.

Once your emergency fund is fully funded, you should stop adding to the account and try your best to forget it's there until you need it. There are only three times when I recommend that people think about their emergency fund:

- You don't have an emergency fund yet, and you're trying to set aside enough money to cover three to six months of expenses.

- You have a legitimate financial emergency and need to access the account. This will happen from time to time, and you shouldn't feel guilty for dipping into the emergency fund if needed. Just make sure to replenish it when the storm passes.

- Once a year, or whenever you have a significant life change that alters your budget (having kids, buying a house, etc.), you should review the size of your emergency fund to make sure it is still sufficient to cover three to six months of spending.

Insurance

Adequate insurance coverage is a critical component of increasing your family's financial security. It's never a fun topic to think about but ensuring that you have adequate levels of coverage in place to protect your family is critical.

There are several types of insurance coverage to consider adding to your family's Marriage-Centered Financial Plan. Some of these are essential, and some are less important. Here are the types of policies that I recommend most couples strongly consider:

Health Insurance: This one is a necessity. You need to have health insurance coverage for you, your spouse, and your kids.

We've talked a lot about how to make the decision on whether to combine finances with your spouse. In that context, it's worth noting that deciding whether you should put your spouse on your health insurance plan is very different from deciding to combine your checking accounts.

I've met some couples who decided not to combine *any* financial accounts but agreed that they both should be on Spouse A's health insurance plan. And I've met a *ton* of couples who combine most or all of their financial accounts but opted to keep separate health insurance.

When picking whose health insurance to use, you should consider:

- The difference in coverage between the options, and

- The difference in premiums.

The trend of late is for it to cost a *lot* more to add a spouse to your health insurance plan, to the point where from a cost savings perspective, it often makes sense to keep separate health insurance policies unless one of you doesn't have access to health insurance through work (or one of you has particularly terrible insurance options).

This isn't a universal rule—there are plenty of exceptions, and this is subject to change in the future. But in the context of deciding whether and to what extent you want to integrate finances with your partner, health insurance is worth reviewing, even though it might not make sense to combine.

Life Insurance: Not every couple needs to have life insurance—particularly right after you get married—but once you buy a home, have kids, or are the sole income earner for your family, it becomes a critical component of your family's financial security.

The challenge is that the longer you wait to get a life insurance policy in place, the higher the annual premium will be. And while health insurance companies are required to guarantee coverage for "pre-existing conditions," life insurance companies are *not* required to do so until you have a policy in force. So, if you wait a few years to apply for a policy and you have an adverse medical diagnosis, you may lose your ability to get a life insurance policy in place (or it may cost you a *lot* more). So, I usually recommend couples get their life insurance coverage in place shortly after getting married.

How much coverage you need is highly variable on the details of your financial situation. Historically, the standard industry rule of thumb is that you should have 10x your annual income in life insurance coverage. So, if your salary is $120,000, you should have a $1,200,000 life insurance policy. But I usually recommend a minimum coverage amount of $250,000–$500,000, depending on your financial situation. (Remember, if you're a stay-at-home parent, you might not provide the income, but if something were to happen to you, your spouse would need to hire some help for the kids! You need life insurance, too!)

In the vast majority of situations, you should get **term life insurance** rather than permanent life insurance. A term insurance policy is only good for a certain amount of time. If you outlive the term of the policy, you stop paying premiums, and your coverage goes away. In turn, the premiums are a *lot* less than they are for permanent life insurance policies (which are guaranteed to pay your beneficiaries the death benefit no matter when you die).

The goal of life insurance is not to need to use it. If your life insurance ends up being a waste of money, that's a *good* thing. And if you have a solid Marriage-Centered Financial Plan in place, there will likely be a time when you don't actually *need* life insurance anymore!

Still, you want to make sure you have the insurance coverage in place until your youngest child is through college. If you haven't had kids yet (or are intending to have additional children), this would mean your term insurance policy should be at least twenty years.

And, of course, a life insurance policy you get for yourself only covers your life (and would pay the benefit to your spouse if something were to happen to you). Your spouse needs to have their own term life insurance policy as well!

Disability Insurance: This insurance is often overlooked but can be a critical part of your family's financial security plan. Long-term disability insurance is designed to protect your income in the event you are unable to work due to an illness or disability.

Most young couples I talk to tend to dismiss the likelihood that they need this sort of insurance, but the data suggests otherwise. According to a June 2020 actuarial report from the Social Security

Administration, "For a … worker born in 2000, the probability of becoming disabled between age 20 and normal retirement age is 25 percent, and the probability of dying between age 20 and normal retirement age is 13 percent." According to the data, young people are twice as likely to need to file a disability insurance claim as they are to file a life insurance claim.

Disability insurance doesn't just cover the types of things you'd typically think of when you hear the word "disability." If you work at a desk job, your policy would cover you if you were to break your hand and be unable to type for several months. If you get a cancer diagnosis and need to miss time at work while you undergo treatment, your disability insurance policy would cover you.

A standard disability insurance policy will pay you anywhere between 40% and 80% of your monthly income when you file a claim and will continue to pay until your standard retirement age or until you recover. There is typically a waiting period between when you become disabled and when you start receiving the benefits, called an "elimination period," that can range anywhere from three months to two years. One way to make these policies more affordable is by increasing your emergency fund (which you could use to support yourself during the elimination period) and increasing the elimination period.

Most US workers are covered by Social Security Disability Insurance (SSDI), but it is *exceptionally* hard to qualify to receive benefits under SSDI. I typically don't recommend relying on SSDI for your disability insurance coverage, as there are a *lot* of disabilities that wouldn't qualify you to receive benefits under SSDI.

Many employers offer long-term disability insurance as an employee benefit, with the most common coverage level being sixty percent of your income. One thing to keep in mind, though, is that unless you are paying the disability insurance premiums yourself, the benefits will be considered taxable income when you get them— meaning the sixty percent of your income paid as a benefit under the policy will look a little more like forty percent of your income by the time you pay taxes on the benefit. Getting a disability insurance policy on your own will require you to pay the premiums of the policy, but it would result in you getting the benefits tax-free. Not to mention, if you leave your job and are relying on the disability insurance coverage through the job, you typically will lose this coverage when you leave. It might cost more to get a separate policy, but there are a lot of benefits to doing so.

There is one other important note on disability insurance policies you should pay attention to. Once you get better and can go back to work, the policy will stop paying benefits, as you might expect. But what constitutes "going back to work" can vary from policy to policy:

- Some policies will only pay you until you can go back to work in *any* job you could reasonably be expected to qualify for.

- Other policies will pay you until you are well enough to go back to work in your chosen career field.

This second type of policy—called an "own occupation" disability insurance policy—is the better type, especially if you are a high-income earner or have a lot of specialized knowledge that you use in your career.

Disability insurance is complicated, and I recommend that you seek the opinion of an expert (from someone who doesn't sell disability insurance for a living) to make sure you have the right type of policy for your situation. But it's something I recommend for most couples that usually isn't in the front of people's minds.

Other Types of Insurance to Consider: Health, life, and disability are the big and most complicated types of insurance policies I recommend for most couples. But there are certainly other types of insurance that you should consider, including:

- **Auto Insurance:** Obviously, this is one you need if you own or drive a car. Be sure to periodically review the coverage levels of the policy to make sure you are sufficiently covered with liability protection as your net worth increases.

- **Renter's or Homeowner's Insurance:** Again, everyone needs either renter's or homeowner's insurance. If you're renting your home, you should get renter's insurance to give you liability protection and protect the value of your belongings. Every year or two, you should periodically increase the value of your property protected under the policy to make sure you could replace your belongings in the event something happens to your apartment. For homeowner's insurance, the same thing applies—you should periodically increase the replacement value amount of the policy to make sure that your policy's coverage keeps up with inflation.

- **Umbrella Insurance:** For high-income earners or high-net-worth couples, I highly recommend getting an umbrella insurance policy to give you extra protection against legal liability. These policies are very inexpensive and give you a lot of extra protection from lawsuits.

Prenuptial Agreements[15]

I'll say off the bat that this is a very emotionally complicated subject for some couples to address. If either you or your partner feels strongly about having a prenup in place, you should go back and work through the exercises and techniques covered in Part 2 to help you come to a resolution.

Generally, I don't recommend that couples get prenup agreements unless there are significant financial differences between members of the couple. If you and your spouse have about the same amount of financial assets, roughly equal incomes, and your financial situation is very straightforward, you probably don't need a prenup. The primary purpose of a prenup is to specify how financial assets would be

---

15. This section talks about prenup agreements, which, by definition, are put in place before you get married. But it is possible to get a "postnup" agreement in place as well.

divided up in the event of a divorce. If you're roughly equal financially, there probably isn't a strong need to have a prenup since the baseline assumption in many states is that things would be divided up relatively evenly.

There are a few circumstances where a prenup might make sense:

One of you owns a home prior to the marriage: If one of you bought a home on your own before you got married, you should have a proactive discussion about what would happen to the home if things don't work out.

Extreme differences in wealth or income: If you barely have $100 to your name and marry a multi-millionaire, this can create challenging relationship dynamics for you and your spouse as you start to combine households. The good news is that the Marriage-Centered Financial Planning process will help you navigate these dynamics to minimize the risks of your financial differences undermining the strength of your marriage. But for peace of mind and to help set the table for these conversations, it's worth considering a prenup to specify what would happen to wealth that was built prior to the marriage.

Extreme differences in family wealth: This might not even have anything to do with your spouse, but if you're marrying into a very wealthy family, this family wealth can create challenging relationship dynamics with your spouse's family. Challenging relationship dynamics with your in-laws is something *everyone* might face from time to time. But if you're marrying a Vanderbilt or Rockefeller or Bush or Clinton, there are dynamics at play of a completely different magnitude. A prenup can be a great tool to help you navigate these relationship dynamics to take the issue off the table.

If you've been married before—and especially if you have children from a prior marriage: Prenups can be an important tool to guarantee certain assets are set off the table for the benefit of your children from your first marriage.

Work together with your spouse to determine if a prenup makes sense for your family, being sure to pay attention to your family's mission statement and the Four Horsemen along the way.

Cohabitation Agreements

This one is only relevant for couples who aren't married and either own a home together, or one partner owns the home and is essentially renting part of it to their partner. To give you and your partner legal protection in the event of a breakup, I recommend working with an attorney to get a cohabitation agreement in place to specify the terms under which you would dissolve the household and sell the home.

Estate Planning Documents

The final piece of your financial security plan should include an estate plan that specifies what happens to your financial assets when you pass away or become incapacitated. There are several things to pay attention to here:

Get a will (or create a trust-based estate plan): I could probably write an entire book on the ins and outs of how to set up an estate plan. For this discussion, understand that you can have either a will-based estate plan or a trust-based estate plan. The trust-based option is the better one on paper, but it's significantly more complicated to implement correctly. If you're a high-income or high-net-worth couple, it's worth paying the extra money and putting in the extra legwork to get the full trust-based estate plan in place. But for many people, a will-based estate plan is sufficient, at least at first. Whatever you do, just get *something* in place after you get married and *especially* once you have kids. You can always "upgrade" your estate plan down the road as your financial situation changes.

Specify a guardian for your children: This one is pretty straightforward. If you have kids, make sure that your estate plan includes guardianship documents so that if something happens to you, there's no question about where your little ones will go.

Update your beneficiaries: Update relevant beneficiaries on your retirement accounts and life insurance. Here's a fun fact: any account that has a beneficiary (most commonly retirement accounts and life insurance policies) *doesn't* pass through your will—it goes right to your beneficiaries. This means if you get a will in place that leaves everything to your spouse, but the beneficiary of a 401(k) from your first job you had before you got married is your sister, the 401(k) is going to go to your sister—regardless of what your will says. So, you should periodically go through each of your accounts and make sure that the beneficiary is your spouse. When you have kids, you should add a secondary or "contingent" beneficiary as specified in your will so that the accounts go to your kids if something were to happen to both you and your spouse.

FINANCIAL FREEDOM COMPONENTS OF A MARRIAGE-CENTERED FINANCIAL PLAN

Once you have identified the financial security components you and your spouse want to implement in your Marriage-Centered Financial Plan, the rest of your financial assets and/or monthly savings can be directed toward your other goals. One of these goals should be a retirement or financial freedom goal. Even if you don't intend to retire in the traditional sense, you should be saving and investing your money for the future in some capacity.

In some ways, the components of the financial freedom part of your plan are more straightforward to discuss. "All" you need to be doing to work toward retirement is consistently investing a portion of your income and any money you have on hand not earmarked for your short-term goals or emergency fund. Typically, I recommend investing somewhere between ten and twenty percent of your income for retirement, depending on how much you're looking to spend in retirement and how much you already have saved.

But much like the estate planning items in the last section, investing is a complicated subject to discuss that could warrant a book on its own. Here are a few principles-based concepts to get you started on your investing journey:

Use Tax-Advantaged Accounts Whenever Possible

Managing your tax bill in the early stages of your career is relatively straightforward, but as you start to build retirement assets and prepare for how to transition from saving for retirement to living in retirement, having a plan for how to manage taxes on your investment accounts becomes very important.

Generally, retirement accounts come in two different "flavors," and whether you pay taxes now or later depends on the flavor that you choose:

- *Traditional* retirement accounts (traditional 401(k), traditional 403(b), traditional IRA, etc.) are accounts where you can generally deduct the contributions you make to the accounts now (to save on taxes today), but you'll be taxed on the money when it's withdrawn in retirement.

- *Roth* retirement accounts (Roth 401(k), Roth 403(b), Roth IRA, etc.) are accounts where you make after-tax contributions now (for which you don't get a tax break today), but the account can be accessed tax-free when you retire.

The decision to choose the Traditional or Roth option, then, comes down to when you expect your tax rate to be higher.[16]

If you think your tax rate will be higher today than it will be when you retire, you should take the tax deduction today by using the Traditional retirement accounts and pay taxes at a lower rate when you withdraw the money in retirement.

If you expect your tax rate will be higher in retirement than it is today, you should take the tax hit today by using the Roth option and letting your accounts grow tax-free.

This isn't a precise science because not only do we not know how

---

16. There are a number of limits, rules, and regulations that dictate whether you are eligible to make contributions to both Traditional and Roth retirement accounts. Please do your research or consult with an expert to confirm your eligibility before making contributions (or attempting to deduct contributions) to these types of accounts.

high your income will be in retirement, but we also don't know how Congress will change tax rates in the coming decades. That being said, as of the time of this writing, we are at record low tax rates, so I think it's somewhat likely that tax rates will go up from where they are today at some point in the next few decades, making Roth retirement accounts a great option for people in the first half of their careers.

And if you're not sure, there's no harm in splitting the proverbial baby and using both. By putting some money in traditional retirement accounts and some in Roth accounts, you're getting some tax benefits today while also setting aside some tax-free income for retirement.

Here is one final note on tax-advantaged accounts. While this discussion primarily has focused on retirement, there are other tax-advantaged accounts out there that you should take advantage of if it makes sense in the context of your Marriage-Centered Financial Plan. Specifically, if saving for your kid's college is an important priority in your family's mission statement, utilizing a 529 or Coverdell investment account is a great way to grow your money tax-free for education. And if you have a High-Deductible Health Insurance plan (HDHP), utilizing a Health Savings Account (HSA) combines the best tax features of the traditional and Roth investment accounts. In other words, you can deduct contributions to your HSA *and* withdraw the money tax-free (as long as you use the proceeds for qualifying medical expenses).

Invest in (Almost) Everything

You likely have heard you should diversify your investments to avoid putting your proverbial eggs in the same hypothetical basket. That is 100% true.

Ideally, you'll invest money you've earmarked for retirement and other long-term savings goals[17] in a series of investment funds covering almost every aspect of the global economy. My lawyer generally

---

17. Due to the potential for investment volatility in the short term, I do not recommend investing money that you intend to use in the next few years.

doesn't like me to give specific investment recommendations to wide groups of people without knowing the details of their financial circumstances—so I need to keep this section relatively general. These are the types of investment funds you should consider:

- Large US Company Funds
- Small US Company Funds
- International Stock Funds
- US Government Bond Funds
- International Bond Funds
- Corporate Bond Funds
- Real Estate Funds

You don't necessarily need all of these in every single account you own, and each of these categories has unique risks. But you should consider having investment exposure in all of these areas.

One final note: Notice that I use the word "funds" here rather than "stocks." In order to minimize investment risk, I recommend avoiding investing in individual company stocks in the vast majority of your investment portfolio. If you want to have a little money set aside to dabble in investing in individual company stocks, that's okay, but your serious money should be at work in a diversified investment portfolio.

While "financial security" and "financial freedom" often manifest as opposite concepts in personal finance, they ultimately need to work together. A good Marriage-Centered Financial Plan will address *both* of these concepts by ensuring you have a stable and secure financial foundation built for your family through having an emergency fund, adequate insurance protection, and the right estate planning documents in place, and then investing (almost) everything else for your longer-term goals.

But at the end of the day, the most effective vehicle for achieving financial security *and* financial freedom for your family doesn't have to do with emergency funds or insurance or investments at all.

The best way to protect your family's financial security and achieve long-term financial freedom is by investing in your marriage. By having your marriage be the center of your financial plan, you are protecting your most important asset and increasing the likelihood that you realize the vision you created in your mission statement and achieve your most deeply held financial goals.

Conclusion

In January 1964, The Beatles were feeling the pressure.

A few months earlier, they had released their fifth single, *I Want to Hold Your Hand.* To say that it was a success would be an understatement. The song was well on its way to being their bestselling single ever—it was at the top of the charts in the UK and was their first song ever to hit #1 in the United States.

And their record label was ready for the Fab Four to crank out their next hit.

In between shows in France, John Lennon and Paul McCartney sat down to write a song they hoped would be that next big hit. A few months later, the world was introduced to the Beatles' sixth single, *Can't Buy Me Love.*

It's a nice sentiment. But is it true? Can money actually buy you love?

No! No, it can't. Of course, money can't literally buy you love. Paul McCartney wasn't a financial planner, but he definitely got the lyrics right!

Money doesn't buy love, and money won't fix a broken relationship.

But learning to manage your money well together will make your marriage stronger.

By making it to the end of this book, you now have the tools you need to implement your own Marriage-Centered Financial Plan with your spouse. You've come a long way, and the only thing left to do is to start implementing what you've learned.

Making the types of changes we've discussed in this book isn't always easy, but don't give up. Your financial bottom line—and your marriage—will thank you.

If I were to ask you to close your eyes and picture a status symbol, what comes to mind?

For some people, it might be a Maserati or a Lamborghini. Others might picture a Rolex watch or a Louis Vuitton handbag.

For decades, Americans have spent money to acquire symbols that give impressions of wealth, status, and power.

There's nothing *wrong* with any of these things, per se, if you're acquiring them for the right reasons (and as long as you can afford them). But in my opinion, there are far better status symbols than a car, jewelry, or a nice home.

Through a Marriage-Centered Financial Planning lens, none of these items are true status symbols.

Instead, the biggest and best status symbol is a long-term marriage.

It's not something that can be bought or paid for. It's not something that only happens if you're lucky or if you're part of the one percent.

A good, healthy, long-term marriage is something that *any* couple can achieve... but it's something that must be earned. For a marriage to flourish, it requires commitment, honesty, vulnerability, devotion, and love. It requires you to think not just of your own interests but also those of your spouse. It requires you to grow with your spouse as life throws you curveballs.

There's a *lot* more to a successful marriage than learning to manage money effectively together... but doing so will be invaluable to you on your journey to attain this greatest status symbol.

You know how to make it happen. Now it's time to get it done!

Acknowledgments

There are *so* many people I want to thank for helping and inspiring me on the journey to publishing this book.

First and most importantly, to my wife, Mary Kathryn. While some of the concepts and frameworks I teach in this book have come from my work experience or formal education in the fields of money and marriage, many of these concepts were developed as a result of things I've learned in our marriage over the past several years. Thank you for always supporting me and being patient during the long evening and weekend hours it took to produce this book. I love you, and I appreciate you more than I can say.

To my parents, Bill and Debra, and my sister Katie: thank you so much for your unconditional love and support. So much of the way we handle money comes from the way we were raised, and I am no exception to that rule. I am incredibly fortunate to have had my family set such a positive example for me to follow.

My journey to fully embrace my goal of being *the* financial planner for couples who need help navigating difficult financial and marital decisions has been a long and incredibly rewarding one. For the past three years, my financial planner BFF Heather Townsend has been pushing me nearly every week to embrace Marriage-Centered Financial Planning as my true calling. Thank you, Heather...and I'm sorry I fought back for so long!

Positive peer pressure can go a long, long way to helping you achieve your goals. Thank you to three great friends for pushing me (and one great friend who quite literally coerced me) to finish this project: Brian Miller, Kellie Lancaster, Gabrielle-Ann Torre, and Liane Sullivan. (I promised Gabrielle that the coercer shall not be named.)

On the technical side, it quite literally took a village to move this book from a concept in my head to a published work. Thank you to the many, many people who helped me to produce this book. These include: David Grandouiller and Yasmin Gruss (editors), Lauren Crane (graphic designer), Steve Kuhn (cover and interior designer), Johanna Leigh (proofreader), and Allison Harpole and Peggy Bills (marketing support). I also want to extend a special thank you to Dr. Megan McCoy, Kellie Lancaster, and Erin Keeley for agreeing to be interviewed during the early stages of the book writing process.

I had an incredibly difficult time coming up with the right name and cover design for this book. To the people who provided feedback on the book name and/or cover design, thank you *so* much for helping steer me in the right direction. This includes nearly everyone mentioned in this acknowledgment section already, as well as the following people: Lorenzo Cabantog, Jane Caudell-Feagan, Abby Cubbison, Stephanie Dillemuth, Tom Halley, Anna Hannan, Jack Hannan, Amanda Karch, Samantha Macario, Lindsay McDonnell, Dr. Alex Melkumian, Joseph Mercado, Nora O'Brien, Kevin Steele, and Hayley Trahan-Liptak.

Finally, to each and every single one of my clients: thank you for the trust you've placed in me and the ways you've inspired me since I launched Pacesetter Planning back in November 2016. I am incredibly lucky to help an amazing group of clients through the good times and the bad. You are the reason I do the work that I do and why I could never imagine doing anything else.

Notes

INTRODUCTION

"A TD Bank Study in 2019 found ..." "2019 Love & Money Survey." *TD Bank*, https://stories.td.com/us/en/article/2019-love-money-survey. Accessed 10 February 2021.

"That same TD Bank study found that..." Ibid.

"A study by Ally Bank in 2018 ..." Gene King. "Money Causes the Most Stress for Couples, According to New Ally Survey." *Ally Bank*, https://media.ally.com/2018-06-12-Money-Causes-the-Most-Stress-for-Couples-According-to-New-Ally-Survey. Accessed 10 February 2021.

"A landmark study in the Family Relationships..." Dew, Jeffrey, Sonya Britt, and Sandra Huston. "Examining the Relationship Between Financial Issues and Divorce." *Family Relationships: Interdisciplinary Journal of Applied Family Science*, Volume 61 Issue 4, 2012. Pages 615-628. Accessed 10 February 2021.

CHAPTER 1

"Dr. Glen Gabbard, psychiatrist at Baylor University..." Gabbard, Glen O. Editorial review on cover, *Money Talks: in Therapy, Society, and Life*, edited by Brenda Berger and Stephanie Newman, Routledge, 2012.

"In *Money Talks – in Therapy, Society, and...* "Berger, Brenda and Stephanie Newman. *Money Talks: in Therapy, Society, and Life*. Routledge, 2012.

CHAPTER 2

"Case in point: A study conducted by ..." Boren, Zachary Davies. "Talking about money is Britain's last taboo." *The Independent*, https://www.independent.co.uk/news/science/talking-about-money-is-britain-s-last-taboo-10508902.html. Accessed 4 November 2020.

CHAPTER 4

"In his research, Dr. Gottman found that ..." Lisitsa, Ellie. "The Four Horsemen: Criticism, Contempt, Defensiveness, and Stonewalling." *The Gottman Institute,* https://www.gottman.com/blog/the-four-horsemen-recognizing-criticism-contempt-defensiveness-and-stonewalling/. Accessed 17 November 2020.

"Dr Gottman's Four Horsemen" (Entire section). Lisitsa, Ibid.

CHAPTER 5

"Money Scripts" (Entire section): Klontz, Brad, Sonya L. Britt, Jennifer Mentzer, and Ted Klontz. "Money Beliefs and Financial Behaviors: Development of the Klontz Money Script Inventory." *The Journal of Financial Therapy*, Volume 2 Issue 1, 2011. Accessed 13 September 2021.

"Money Scripts" (Entire section): "Your Money Script." *Your Mental Wealth Advisors,* https://www.yourmentalwealthadvisors.com/our-process/your-money-script/. Accessed 13 September 2021.

"Money Scripts" (Entire section): Klontz, Brad, Rick Kahler, and Ted Klontz. *Facilitating Financial Health: Tools for Financial Planners, Coaches, and Therapists.* The National Underwriter Company, 2016, Chapters 6 and 7.

CHAPTER 6

"I learned this metaphor and framework of 'diagnosing ... '" Richards, Carl. "Financial Prescriptions Shouldn't Be Taken Lightly." *The New York Times,* https://www.nytimes.com/2015/04/14/your-money/financial-prescriptions-shouldnt-be-taken-lightly.html. Accessed 11 March 2021.

"It's *completely* normal for you to have different ..." Rick, Scott I., Deborah A. Small, and Eli J. Finkel. "Fatal (Fiscal) Attraction: Spendthrifts and Tightwads in Marriage." *Journal of Marketing Research*, Volume 48 Issue 2, 2011. Pages 228-237. Accessed 15 June 2022.

"Men and women tend to get different ..." Furnham, Adrian, Sophie von Stumm, and Mark Fenton-O'Creevy. "Sex Differences in Money Pathology in the General Population." *Social Indicators Research,* Volume 123 Issue 3, 2015. Accessed 15 June 2022.

"When She Makes More. Personal finance expert ..." Torabi, Farnoosh. *When She Makes More: The Truth About Navigating Love and Life for a New Generation of Women.* Penguin, 2015.

CHAPTER 7

"Allow me to illustrate how most people ..." Berman, Lee Jay. "The Orange Story." *Santa Monica Business Journal,* May 1996. *Mediation Tools,* http://www.mediationtools.com/articles/smbj9605.html. Accessed 18 May 2021.

"According to the Thomas-Kilmann Conflict Mode Instrument..." Thomas, Kenneth W. and Ralph H. Kilmann. "Thomas-Kilmann Conflict Mode Instrument Profile and Interpretive Report." Xicom, 2007. https://www.researchgate.net/profile/Ralph-Kilmann/publication/265565339_Thomas-Kilmann_conflict_MODE_instrument/links/558c15d908aee43bf6ae1917/Thomas-Kilmann-conflict-MODE-instrument.pdf. Accessed 18 May 2021.

"Setting the Stage for Financial Conflict Resolution" (whole section): Asebedo, Sarah D. "Building Financial Peace: A Conflict Resolution Framework for Money Arguments." *Journal of Financial Therapy*, Volume 7 Issue 2, 2016. Accessed 18 May 2021.

"Resolving Money Arguments" (whole section): Asebedo, Ibid.

CHAPTER 8

"A study conducted by researchers at the ..." Jeanfreau, Michelle M., Kenji Noguchi, Michael D. Mong, and Hans Stadthagen-Gonzalez. "Financial Infidelity in Couple Relationships." *Journal of Financial Therapy*, Volume 9 Issue 1, 2018. Accessed 18 May 2021.

"Some specific examples include a spouse ..." Postmus, Judy L., Sara-Beth Plummer, and Amanda M. Stylianou. "Measuring Economic Abuse in the Lives of Survivors: Revising the Scale of Economic Abuse." *Violence Against Women*, Volume 22 Issue 6, 2015. Accessed 15 June 2022.

CHAPTER 9

"If you review Dunkin's mission statement..." "About Us." *Dunkin*, https://www.dunkindonuts.com/en/about/about-us. Accessed 15 June 2022.

"When you go into a Starbucks, there ..." "Our Company." *Starbucks*, https://www.starbucks.com/about-us/. Accessed 15 June 2022.

"Why is money important to you?" Richards, Carl. *The One Page Financial Plan: A Simple Way to be Smart About Your Money*. Penguin, 2015.

"Question One: Imagine you won the lottery ..." "Moneyeditor." "3 Questions That Will Get Your Finances – And Life – On Track." 31 January 2015. *Money*, https://money.com/collection-post/3-questions-will-put-your-finances-life-right-track/. Accessed 11 March 2021.

"Question Two: Imagine you went to the ..." Money.com, Ibid.

"Question Three: Imagine you learned that you ..." Money.com, Ibid.

" ... there are several common items that tend ..." Kitces, Michael, host. "Why Life Planning Is Simply Financial Planning Done Right with George Kinder." *Financial Advisor Success Podcast*, Episode 15, Kitces.com, 11 April 2017, https://www.kitces.com/blog/george-kinder-institute-life-planning-podcast-seven-stages-maturity/.

" … key elements of the financial conflict resolution framework" Asebedo, Ibid.

CHAPTER 10

" … financial goals as your 'best guess … '" Richards, Carl. "Goals are only guesses." *Behavior Gap,* https://behaviorgap.com/goals-are-only-guesses/. Accessed 11 March 2021.

CHAPTER 11

"According to a 2018 Bank of America Study …" "2018 Better Money Habits Millennial Report, Winter 2018." *Bank of America,* https://bettermoneyhabits.bankofamerica. com/content/dam/bmh/pdf/ar6vnln9-boa-bmh-millennial-report-winter-2018-final2. pdf. Accessed 15 June 2022.

"The book primarily focuses on relationship dynamics …" Torabi, Ibid.

CHAPTER 12

" … approach budgeting as an act of awareness …" Richards, Carl. "The Solution to Maintaining a Budget is Awareness." *Behavior Gap,* https://behaviorgap.com/the-solution-to-maintaining-a-budget-is-awareness/. Accessed 18 May 2021.

CHAPTER 14

"The move focuses on the Smith family …" Minnelli, Vincente, et al. *Meet Me in St. Louis.* Burbank, CA: Distributed by Warner Home Video, 2004.

CHAPTER 16

"According to a June 2020 actuarial report …" United States. Social Security Administration, Office of the Chief Actuary. *Disability and Death Probability Tables for Insured Workers Born in 2000.* Social Security Administration, June 2020. https://www.ssa.gov/oact/NOTES/ran6/an2020-6.pdf. Accessed 9 November 2021.

CONCLUSION

"A few months later, the world was …" The Beatles. "Can't Buy Me Love." *Spotify.* https://open.spotify.com/album/7vEJAtP3KgKSpOHVgwm3Eh?highlight=spotify:track:38Vb1J5W5LOs0i7SAF76pa.